THE BOTTOM BILLION

The Bottom Billion

*Why the Poorest Countries Are Failing
and What Can Be Done About It*

PAUL COLLIER

OXFORD

UNIVERSITY PRESS

2007

OXFORD
UNIVERSITY PRESS

Oxford University Press, Inc., publishes works that further
Oxford University's objective of excellence
in research, scholarship, and education.

Oxford   New York
Auckland   Cape Town   Dar es Salaam   Hong Kong   Karachi
Kuala Lumpur   Madrid   Melbourne   Mexico City   Nairobi
New Delhi   Shanghai   Taipei   Toronto

With offices in
Argentina   Austria   Brazil   Chile   Czech Republic   France   Greece
Guatemala   Hungary   Italy   Japan   Poland   Portugal   Singapore
South Korea   Switzerland   Thailand   Turkey   Ukraine   Vietnam

Copyright © 2007 by Paul Collier

Published by Oxford University Press, Inc.
198 Madison Avenue, New York, New York 10016
www.oup.com

Oxford is a registered trademark of Oxford University Press

Library of Congress Cataloging-in-Publication Data
Collier, Paul.
The bottom billion : why the poorest countries are failing and what
can be done about it / by Paul Collier.
p. cm.
ISBN 978-0-19-531145-7 (cloth)
1. Poor—Developing countries. 2. Poverty—Developing countries   I. Title.
HC79.P6C634 2007
338.9009172'4—dc22   2006036630

7 9 8
Printed in the United States of America
on acid-free paper

For Daniel: his world

Contents

Preface   *ix*

Part 1   *What's the Issue?*

   1. Falling Behind and Falling Apart:
     The Bottom Billion   *3*

Part 2   *The Traps*

   2. The Conflict Trap   *17*
   3. The Natural Resource Trap   *38*
   4. Landlocked with Bad Neighbors   *53*
   5. Bad Governance in a Small Country   *64*

Part 3   *An Interlude: Globalization to the Rescue?*

   6. On Missing the Boat: The Marginalization
     of the Bottom Billion in the World Economy   *79*

Part 4   *The Instruments*

   7. Aid to the Rescue?   *99*
   8. Military Intervention   *124*
   9. Laws and Charters   *135*
   10. Trade Policy for Reversing Marginalization   *157*

Part 5   *The Struggle for the Bottom Billion*

11. An Agenda for Action   *175*

Research on Which This Book Is Based   *193*

Index   *197*

Preface

I WAS A STUDENT at Oxford in 1968. I remember joining something called the Oxford Revolutionary Socialist Students, a name now beyond parody. But it all seemed simple then. When I graduated I wanted to put my knowledge of economics to use in Africa. Africa's new countries were ill-equipped, and scarcely any Africans had received the sort of education I had just been through. At the time many Oxford students had family connections with Africa, as their fathers had been colonial administrators. Not in my case—my father was a butcher in Yorkshire. But some of those colonial connections must have rubbed off on me: the father of my friend had been the governor general of a little country called Nyasaland, and so I read up on it. What I read made me resolve to go there. Renamed Malawi, it was the poorest country on the continent. It is easier to rename countries than to change them: thirty-five years later it is still as dirt poor as it was then. In another thirty-five years I doubt it will be much different, unless . . . This book is about that "unless."

Malawi hasn't changed much in the last thirty-five years, and in one sense neither have I: I'm still working on Africa, now as a professor at Oxford. In between I've been a professor at Harvard, and directed the World Bank's research department, where I was brought in by Joe Stiglitz to strengthen its focus on the poorest countries. Indeed, my first assignment for the World Bank was to go with Joe to Ethiopia. Since I had just married, the trip was my honeymoon, but with Joe instead of my wife. Fortunately, she was understanding—whether by coincidence or the attraction of like minds, after university she had worked in Malawi.

This book is about the Malawis and the Ethiopias of this world, the minority of developing countries that are now at the bottom of the global economic system. Some, such as Malawi, have always been at the bottom. Others, including Sierra Leone, once were less poor than India or China. The countries now at the bottom are distinctive not just in being the poorest but also in having failed to grow. They are not following the development path of most other nations; they are adrift. As once-poor India and China, and countries like them, surged ahead, the global poverty picture has been confused, concealing this divergent pattern. Of course, for some countries to do relatively better, others must do relatively worse. But the decline of the countries now at the bottom is not just relative; often it is absolute. Many of these countries are not just falling behind, they are falling apart.

For the past few years much of my work has been on civil war. I wanted to understand why conflict was increasingly concentrated in low-income Africa. Gradually, I developed the notion of the "conflict trap." It shows how certain economic conditions make a country prone to civil war, and how, once conflict has started, the cycle of violence becomes a trap from which it is difficult to escape. I realized that the conflict trap was one explanation for the countries now at the bottom of the world economy. But it was not the whole story. Malawi has been conflict-free for its entire postindependence history, yet it still has not developed. Neither have Kenya and Nigeria, countries on which at different stages in my career I wrote books, and which looked neither like Malawi nor like each other. Nor do I believe that poverty itself is a trap. These development failures occurred against a backdrop of global development success—poverty is something that most people are managing to escape. Since 1980 world poverty has been falling for the first time in history. Nor was it just a matter of Africa. Elsewhere there were also development failures: countries such as Haiti, Laos, Burma, and the Central Asian countries, of which Afghanistan has been the most spectacular. A one-size-fits-all explanation for development failure doesn't ring true against such diversity.

Part of the reason single-factor theories about development failure are so common is that modern academics tend to specialize: they are trained to produce intense but narrow beams of light. However, in my career I have written books on rural development, labor markets, macroeconomic shocks, investment, and conflict. And for a while I was working for Joe Stiglitz, who really was interested in everything and had something ingenious to say about much of it. This breadth has its advantages. Eventually I came to see that four distinct traps explain the countries now at the bottom. Between them they account for around a billion people. If nothing is done about it, this group will gradually diverge from the rest of the world economy over the next couple of decades, forming a ghetto of misery and discontent.

The problems these countries have are very different from those we have addressed for the past four decades in what we have called "developing countries"—that is, virtually all countries besides the most developed, which account for only one-sixth of the earth's people. For all this time we have defined developing countries so as to encompass five billion of the six billion people in the world. But not all developing countries are the same. Those where development has failed face intractable problems not found in the countries that are succeeding. We have, in fact, done the easier part of global development; finishing the job now gets more difficult. Finish it we must, because an impoverished ghetto of one billion people will be increasingly impossible for a comfortable world to tolerate.

Unfortunately, it is not just about giving these countries our money. If it were, it would be relatively easy because there are not that many of them. With some important exceptions, aid does not work so well in these environments, at least as it has been provided in the past. Change in the societies at the very bottom must come predominantly from within; we cannot impose it on them. In all these societies there are struggles between brave people wanting change and entrenched interests opposing it. To date, we have largely been bystanders in this struggle. We can do much more to strengthen the hand of the reformers. But to do so we will need to draw upon tools— such as military interventions, international standard-setting, and trade policy—that to date have been used for other purposes. The agencies that control these instruments have neither knowledge of nor interest in the problems of the bottom billion. They will need to learn, and governments will need to learn how to coordinate this wide range of policies.

These ideas open horizons across the political divide. The left will find that approaches it has discounted, such as military interventions, trade, and encouraging growth, are critical means to the ends it has long embraced. The right will find that, unlike the challenge of global poverty reduction, the problem of the bottom billion will not be fixed automatically by global growth, and that neglect now will become a security nightmare for the world of our children. We can crack this problem; indeed, we must. But to do so, we need to build a unity of purpose.

To build a unity of purpose, thinking needs to change, not just within the development agencies but among the wider electorates whose views shape what is possible. Without an informed electorate, politicians will continue to use the bottom billion merely for photo opportunities, rather than promoting real transformation. This book is an attempt to shift thinking; it is written to be read, and so I have kept clear of footnotes and the rest of the usual grim apparatus of professional scholarship. I have tried to write something that you can enjoy reading. But don't let that lead you to conclude that what I have to say is just a load of froth. Underpinning the book are a mass of technical papers published in professional journals and subjected to blind refereeing. I list some of them at the end of the book.

Research is often like a quest. You start with a question that sounds impossible to answer: how much aid leaks into military spending, or how much of Africa's wealth has fled the continent. How would you go about answering those questions? Ask each third-world army where it got its money? Knock on the doors of the Swiss banks and ask them to report their African accounts? There is a different way of getting to the answers, and it is statistical. This stands in contrast to the crude images that often provide us with what we think we know about the world. For rebellion, as an example, the image is often that of Che Guevara, ubiquitous in my generation as a poster on student walls. The poster did our thinking for us. Our notions about the problems of the poorest countries are saturated with such images: not just of noble rebels but of starving children, heartless businesses, crooked politicians. You are held prisoner by these images. While you are held prisoner, so are our politicians, because they do what you want. I am going to take you beyond images. Sometimes I am going to smash them. And my image smasher is statistical evidence.

In conducting my statistical analysis I have relied on quite a few young collaborators, many of whom you will meet in the pages that follow. One of them, Anke Hoeffler, has been central to much of this work. We have worked together for a decade, a double act in which I play the role of the impossibly annoying professor, while Anke somehow keeps her temper and presses on. If you want a somewhat exaggerated image of how we work, you could do worse than picture Morse and Lewis from the famous British detective series. As with them, our research usually involves a lot of false starts. However, though like Morse I am based in Oxford, unlike him I work with a highly international group. As you will have guessed, Anke is German. But there are also Måns, who is Swedish; Lisa, who is French; Steve, an Irish American; Cathy, an African American; Victor, from Sierra Leone; and Phil, an Australian. This is only part of a long list, but you get the idea. What they all have in common is the patience to be painstaking and the brains to have mastered difficult skills. Without them, there would have been no book, because there would have been no results on which to base the story. This book is the big picture that emerges when you connect the dots. But the dots are a story in themselves. Although this is not a book about research, I hope that along the way you will get some of the flavor of how modern research is done, and a sense of the thrill that comes from cracking intractable questions.

THE BOTTOM BILLION

Part 1

What's the Issue?

CHAPTER 1

Falling Behind and Falling Apart: The Bottom Billion

THE THIRD WORLD HAS SHRUNK. For forty years the development challenge has been a rich world of one billion people facing a poor world of five billion people. The Millennium Development Goals established by the United Nations, which are designed to track development progress through 2015, encapsulate this thinking. By 2015, however, it will be apparent that this way of conceptualizing development has become outdated. Most of the five billion, about 80 percent, live in countries that are indeed developing, often at amazing speed. The real challenge of development is that there is a group of countries at the bottom that are falling behind, and often falling apart.

The countries at the bottom coexist with the twenty-first century, but their reality is the fourteenth century: civil war, plague, ignorance. They are concentrated in Africa and Central Asia, with a scattering elsewhere. Even during the 1990s, in retrospect the golden decade between the end of the Cold War and 9/11, incomes in this group declined by 5 percent. We must learn to turn the familiar numbers upside down: a total of five billion people who are already prosperous, or at least are on track to be so, and one billion who are stuck at the bottom.

This problem matters, and not just to the billion people who are living and dying in fourteenth-century conditions. It matters to us. The twenty-first-century world of material comfort, global travel, and economic interdependence will become increasingly vulnerable to these large islands of chaos. And it matters now. As the bottom billion diverges from an increasingly sophisticated world economy, integration will become harder, not easier.

And yet it is a problem denied, both by development *biz* and by development *buzz*. Development biz is run by the aid agencies and the companies that get the contracts for their projects. They will fight this thesis with the tenacity of bureaucracies endangered, because they like things the way they are. A definition of development that encompasses five billion people gives them license to be everywhere, or more honestly, everywhere but the bottom billion. At the bottom, conditions are rather rough. Every development agency has difficulty getting its staff to serve in Chad and Laos; the glamour postings are for countries such as Brazil and China. The World Bank has large offices in every major middle-income country but not a single person resident in the Central African Republic. So don't expect the development biz to refocus voluntarily.

Development buzz is generated by rock stars, celebrities, and NGOs. To its credit, it does focus on the plight of the bottom billion. It is thanks to development buzz that Africa gets on the agenda of the G8. But inevitably, development buzz has to keep its messages simple, driven by the need for slogans, images, and anger. Unfortunately, although the plight of the bottom billion lends itself to simple moralizing, the answers do not. It is a problem that needs to be hit with several policies at the same time, some of them counterintuitive. Don't look to development buzz to formulate such an agenda: it is at times a headless heart.

What of the governments of the countries at the bottom? The prevailing conditions bring out extremes. Leaders are sometimes psychopaths who have shot their way to power, sometimes crooks who have bought it, and sometimes brave people who, against the odds, are trying to build a better future. Even the appearance of modern government in these states is sometimes a façade, as if the leaders are reading from a script. They sit at the international negotiating tables, such as the World Trade Organization, but they have nothing to negotiate. The seats stay occupied even in the face of meltdown in their societies: the government of Somalia continued to be officially "represented" in the international arena for years after Somalia ceased to have a functioning government in the country itself. So don't expect the governments of the bottom billion to unite in formulating a practical agenda: they are fractured between villains and heroes, and some of them are barely there. For our future world to be livable the heroes must win their struggle. But the villains have the guns and the money, and to date they have usually prevailed. That will continue unless we radically change our approach.

All societies used to be poor. Most are now lifting out of it; why are others stuck? The answer is traps. Poverty is not intrinsically a trap, otherwise we would all still be poor. Think, for a moment, of development as chutes and ladders. In the modern world of globalization there are some fabulous ladders; most societies are using them. But there are also some chutes, and some societies have hit them. The countries at the bottom are an unlucky minority, but they are stuck.

Traps, and the Countries Caught in Them

Suppose your country is dirt poor, almost stagnant economically, and that few people are educated. You don't have to try that hard to imagine this condition—our ancestors lived this way. With hard work, thrift, and intelligence, a society can gradually climb out of poverty, unless it gets trapped. Development traps have become a fashionable area of academic dispute, with a fairly predictable right-left divide. The right tends to deny the existence of development traps, asserting that any country adopting good policies will escape poverty. The left tends to see global capitalism as inherently generating a poverty trap.

The concept of a development trap has been around for a long time and is most recently associated with the work of the economist Jeffrey Sachs, who has focused on the consequences of malaria and other health problems. Malaria keeps countries poor, and because they are poor the potential market for a vaccine is not sufficiently valuable to warrant drug companies making the huge investment in research that is necessary. This book is about four traps that have received less attention: the conflict trap, the natural resources trap, the trap of being landlocked with bad neighbors, and the trap of bad governance in a small country. Like many developing countries that are now succeeding, all the countries that are the focus of this book are poor. Their distinctive feature is that they got caught in one or another of the traps. These traps are not inescapable, however, and over the years some countries have broken free of them and then started to catch up. Unfortunately, that process of catching up has itself recently stalled. Those countries that have only broken clear of the traps during the last decade have faced a new problem: the global market is now far more hostile to new entrants than it was in the 1980s. The countries newly escaped from the traps may have missed the boat, finding themselves in a limbo-like world in which growth is constrained by external factors; this will be the theme in my discussion of globalization. When Mauritius escaped the traps in the 1980s it rocketed to middle-income levels; when neighboring Madagascar finally escaped the traps two decades later, there was no rocket.

Most countries have stayed clear of any of the traps that are the subject of this book. But countries with a combined population of around one billion people have got caught in them. Underlying that statement are some definitions. For example, one of the traps involves being landlocked— although being landlocked is not sufficient to constitute the trap. But when is a country landlocked? You might think that such a matter is clear enough from an atlas. But what about Zaire, which after the ruinous reign of President Mobutu understandably rebranded itself as the Democratic Republic of the Congo? It is *virtually* landlocked but has a tiny sliver of coast. And Sudan has some coast, but most of its people live far away from it.

In defining these traps I have had to draw lines somewhat arbitrarily, and this creates gray areas. Most developing countries are clearly heading toward success, and others are just as clearly heading toward what might be described as a black hole. For some, however, we really cannot tell. Perhaps Papua New Guinea is heading for success; I hope so, and that is how I have classified it. But there are some experts on Papua New Guinea who would shake their heads in disbelief at that. The judgment calls are inevitably going to be open to challenge. But such challenges do not discredit the underlying thesis: that there is a black hole, and that many countries are indisputably heading into it, rather than being drawn toward success. You will learn more about the fine judgments as the book progresses. For the moment take it on trust that I have drawn the lines defensibly.

Given the way I have drawn the lines, as of 2006 there are around 980 million people living in these trapped countries. Since their populations are growing, by the time you read this the figure will be hovering around the one billion mark. Seventy percent of these people are in Africa, and most Africans are living in countries that have been in one or another of the traps. Africa is therefore the core of the problem. The rest of the world has spotted that. Think of how the international commissions on development have evolved. The first major development commission was established in 1970, led by a former prime minister of Canada. The Pearson Commission took a global focus on development problems. It was followed in 1980 by a commission led by a former chancellor of Germany. The Brandt Commission took the same global focus. By 2005, when Britain's Tony Blair decided to launch a commission on development, the focus had shrunk to Africa: this was a commission *for Africa,* not for development. In 2006 President Horst Köhler of Germany decided that he too would have a development event. He could hardly just repeat Tony Blair—not another Commission for Africa in the very next year. So he called it a forum, but it was still a forum *for Africa.* In reality, however, Africa and the third world are not coterminous. South Africa, for example, is not among the bottom billion—it is manifestly not in the same desperate situation as Chad. Conversely, much of landlocked Central Asia is disturbingly like Chad. So the countries of the bottom billion do not form a group with a convenient geographic label. When I want to use a geographic label for them I describe them as "Africa +," with the + being places such as Haiti, Bolivia, the Central Asian countries, Laos, Cambodia, Yemen, Burma, and North Korea. They all either are still in one of the traps or escaped too late.

I have identified fifty-eight countries that fall into this group, which highlights one typical feature—they are small. Combined, they have fewer people than either India or China. And since their per capita income is also very low, the income of the typical country is negligible, less than that of most rich-world cities. Because this is not company that countries are keen to be in, and because stigmatizing a country tends to create a self-fulfilling prophecy, I will not present a list of these countries. Rather, I will give plenty of examples in each of the traps.

So, how have the countries of the bottom billion been doing? First, consider how people live, or rather die. In the bottom billion average life expectancy is fifty years, whereas in the other developing countries it is sixty-seven years. Infant mortality—the proportion of children who die before their fifth birthday—is 14 percent in the bottom billion, whereas in the other developing countries it is 4 percent. The proportion of children with symptoms of long-term malnutrition is 36 percent in the bottom billion as against 20 percent for the other developing countries.

The Role of Growth in Development

Has this gap between the bottom billion and the rest of the developing world always been there, or has it come about because the bottom billion have been trapped? To find out, we have to disaggregate the statistics that have been used in the past to describe all the countries that we label as "developing." Here's a hypothetical example. Prosperia has a big economy that is growing at 10 percent, but the country has only a small population. Catastrophia is a small economy declining at 10 percent, but it has a large population. The usual approach—employed, for example, by the International Monetary Fund (IMF) in its flagship publication *World Economic Outlook*—is to average figures that relate to the size of a country's economy. On this approach, Prosperia's large, growing economy skews the average upward, and so in aggregate the two countries are described as growing. The problem is that this describes what is going on from the perspective of the typical unit of income, not from the perspective of the typical person. Most units of income are in Prosperia, but most people are in Catastrophia. If we want to describe what the typical person experiences in the countries of the bottom billion, we need to work with figures based not on a country's income but on its population. Does it matter? Well, it does if the poorest countries are diverging from the rest, which is the thesis of this book, because averaging by income dismisses the poorest countries as unimportant. The experience of their people does not count for much precisely because they are poor—their income is negligible.

When we get the data appropriately averaged, what do we find? Those developing countries that are not part of the bottom billion—the middle four billion—have experienced rapid and accelerating growth in per capita income. Let's take it decade by decade. During the 1970s they grew at 2.5 percent a year, hopeful but not remarkable. During the 1980s and 1990s their growth rate accelerated to 4 percent a year. During the first few years of the twenty-first century it accelerated again to over 4.5 percent. These growth rates may not sound sensational, but they are without precedent in history. They imply that children in these countries will grow up to have lives dramatically different from those of their parents. Even where people are still poor, these societies can be suffused with hope: time is on their side.

But how about the bottom billion? Let's again take it decade by decade. During the 1970s their per capita income rose at 0.5 percent a year, so they were becoming slightly better off in absolute terms but at a rate that was likely to be barely perceptible. Given the high degree of volatility of individual incomes in these societies, the slight overall tendency to improvement is likely to have been drowned by these individual risks. The overall tenor of the society will have been dominated by individual fears of falling rather than hope coming from society-wide progress. But in the 1980s the performance of the bottom billion got much worse, *declining* at 0.4 percent a year. In absolute terms, by the end of the 1980s they were back to where they had been in 1970. If you had been living in these societies over that full sweep of twenty years, the only economic experience was of individual volatility: some people went up and some went down. There was no society-wide reason for hope. And then came the 1990s. This is now seen as the golden decade, between the end of the Cold War and 9/11—the decade of the cloudless sky and booming markets. It wasn't so golden for the bottom billion: their rate of absolute decline accelerated to 0.5 percent a year. By the turn of the millennium they were therefore poorer than they had been in 1970.

Is this dismal performance just an artifact of the data? I think that, on the contrary, the genuine problems that afflict the gathering of economic data in the poorest countries are likely overall to have caused an underestimate of their decline. For the countries that have really fallen apart, there are no usable data. For example, the estimated decline among the bottom-billion countries during the 1990s does not include whatever might have been happening in Somalia and Afghanistan. But excluding them is equivalent to assuming that their performance was exactly at the average for the group, and I would be surprised, to say the least, if this was true; I would think it was much worse. In the first four years of the present decade the growth of the bottom billion has picked up to around 1.7 percent, still far below that of the rest of the developing world, but markedly better in absolute terms. Unfortunately, however, this current improvement is likely due to the short-term effects of resource discoveries and high world prices for the natural resources that the bottom billion export. For example, the star growth performer among all the economies of the bottom billion has been Equatorial Guinea. This is a small country of coups and corruption where offshore oil was recently discovered and now dominates income. In sum, even if we were to treat these recent figures as hopeful, which I think would be a misinterpretation, the growth of the bottom billion remains much slower at its peak than even the slowest period of growth in the rest of the developing world and brings them about back to where they were in 1970.

Think about what these two sets of growth rates imply. During the 1970s the bottom billion diverged in growth from the rest of the developing world by 2 percent a year. So even then the main feature of the societies in the bottom billion was divergence, not development. But the situation soon became alarmingly worse. During the 1980s the divergence accelerated to 4.4 percent a year, and during the 1990s it accelerated further to an astonishing 5 percent a year. Taking the three decades as a whole, the experience of the societies in the bottom billion was thus one of massive and accelerating divergence. Given the power of compound growth rates, these differences between the bottom billion and the rest of the developing world will rapidly cumulate into two different worlds. Indeed, the divergence has indeed already pushed most of the countries of the bottom billion to the lowest spot in the global pile.

It was not always that way. Before globalization gave huge opportunities to China and India, they were poorer than many of the countries that have been caught in the traps. But China and India broke free in time to penetrate global markets, whereas other countries that were initially less poor didn't. For the last two decades this has produced a growth pattern that appears confusing. Some initially poor countries are growing very well, and so it can easily look as if there is not really a problem: the bottom appears to be growing as fast as the rest. Over the next two decades the true nature of the problem is going to become apparent, however, because the countries that are trapped in stagnation or decline are now pretty well the poorest. The average person in the societies of the bottom billion now has an income only around one-fifth that of the typical person in the other developing countries, and the gap will just get worse with time. Picture this as a billion people stuck in a train that is slowly rolling backward downhill.

By 2050 the development gulf will no longer be between a rich billion in the most developed countries and five billion in the developing countries; rather, it will be between the trapped billion and the rest of humankind.

So far I have couched the problem of the bottom billion in terms of growth rates: these countries' growth rate has been negative in absolute terms, and in relative terms massively below that of the rest of the developing world. Nowadays, however, the talk is about poverty reduction and the other Millennium Development Goals, not about growth rates. Many of the people who care most about development feel more comfortable talking about goals such as getting girls into school than discussing growth. I share the enthusiasm for getting girls into school, and indeed for all the other goals. But I do not share the discomfort about growth. While I was directing the World Bank's research department, the most controversial paper we produced was one called "Growth Is Good for the Poor." Some NGOs hated it, and it was the only time in five years that Jim Wolfensohn, the Bank's president, phoned me to voice his concern. Yet the central problem of the bottom billion is that they have not grown. The failure of the growth process in these societies simply has to be our core concern, and curing it the core challenge of development. For policies in the rich world to become more supportive of growth in these societies, we will need the full lobbying power of those who care about the world's poor. And so the people who care will need to take another look at growth.

I am definitely not arguing that we should be indifferent to how an economy grows. The growth of Equatorial Guinea, for example, produces benefits for only a handful of its people, but this is exceptional; growth usually does benefit ordinary people. The exaggerated suspicion of growth by those who are concerned about development has manifested itself in the adjectives with which the word *growth* is now routinely encumbered. In strategy documents the word is now generally seen only in the context of the phrase "sustainable, pro-poor growth." Yet overwhelmingly, the problem of the bottom billion has not been that they have had the wrong *type* of growth, it is that they have not had *any* growth. The suspicion of growth has inadvertently undermined genuinely strategic thinking. I remember when one of the world's great experts on banking consulted me because he had been asked to advise one of the countries of the bottom billion. He was struggling to come up with evidence that banking reform would directly help the poorest people in the country, because he sensed that without such evidence his advice would be dismissed. The much stronger evidence that it would help the growth process would not be valued, he felt. Getting growth started in the bottom billion is going to be hard enough even without such hindrances.

We cannot make poverty history unless the countries of the bottom billion start to grow, and they will not grow by turning them into Cuba. Cuba is a stagnant, low-income, egalitarian country with good social services. If the bottom billion emulated Cuba, would this solve their problems? I think that the vast majority of the people living in the bottom billion—and indeed in Cuba—would see it as continued failure. To my mind, development is about giving hope to ordinary people that their children will live in a society that has caught up with the rest of the world. Take that hope away and the smart people will use their energies not to develop their society but to escape from it—as have a million Cubans. Catching up is about radically raising growth in the countries now at the bottom. The fact that stagnation has persisted over such a long period tells us that it is going to be difficult. What can we do beyond caring?

Beyond the Headless Heart: Accepting Complexity

The problem of the bottom billion is serious, but it is fixable. It is much less daunting than the dramatic problems that were overcome in the twentieth century: disease, fascism, and communism. But like most serious problems, it is complicated. Change is going to have to come from within the societies of the bottom billion, but our own policies could make these efforts more likely to succeed, and so more likely to be undertaken.

We will need a range of policy instruments to encourage the countries of the bottom billion to take steps toward change. To date we have used these instruments badly, so there is considerable scope for improvement. The main challenge is that these policy tools span various government agencies, which are not always inclined to cooperate. Traditionally, development has been assigned to aid agencies, which are low in almost every government's pecking order. The U.S. Department of Defense is not going to take advice from that country's Agency for International Development. The British Department of Trade and Industry is not going to listen to the

Department for International Development. To make development policy coherent will require what is termed a "whole-of-government" approach. To get this degree of coordination requires heads of government to focus on the problem. And because success depends on more than just what the United States or any other nation does on its own, it will require joint action across major governments.

The only forum where heads of the major governments routinely meet is the G8. Addressing the problem of the bottom billion is an ideal topic for the G8, but it means using the full range of available policies and so going beyond the Gleneagles agenda of 2005, which was a pledge to double aid programs. Africa is already back on the G8 agenda for the 2007 meeting in Germany. "Africa+" should rightly stay on the G8 agenda until the bottom billion are decisively freed from the development traps. This book sets out an agenda for the G8 that would be effective.

Part 2

The Traps

CHAPTER 2

The Conflict Trap

ALL SOCIETIES HAVE CONFLICT; it is inherent to politics. The problem that is pretty distinctive to the bottom billion is not political conflict but its form. Some of them are stuck in a pattern of violent internal challenges to government. Sometimes the violence is prolonged, a civil war; sometimes it is all over swiftly, a coup d'état. These two forms of political conflict both are costly and can be repetitive. They can trap a country in poverty.

Civil War

Seventy-three percent of people in the societies of the bottom billion have recently been through a civil war or are still in one. Many other countries have had civil wars at one time or another—the United States had one in the nineteenth century, Russia one early in the twentieth century, and Britain one back in the seventeenth—but, as these examples show, wars are not necessarily traps. The American, Russian, and British civil wars were ghastly at the time but were over fairly quickly and were not repeated. For low-income countries, however, the chances of war becoming a trap are much higher. I discovered this working with Anke Hoeffler, a young woman who was initially my doctoral student and is now my colleague. Anke's doctoral thesis was about the sources of growth, then a fashionable topic in economics. One of the factors known to impede growth is war. As I mulled over Anke's work it struck me that it would be interesting to turn the inquiry around: instead of explaining whether a country grew fast or slowly in terms of whether it was at war or peace, we could investigate whether proneness to war was explicable in terms of differences in growth.

Causes of Civil War

So what causes civil war? Rebel movements themselves justify their actions in terms of a catalogue of grievances: repression, exploitation, exclusion. Politically motivated academics have piled in with their own hobbyhorses, which usually cast rebels as heroes. I have come to distrust this discourse of grievance as self-serving. Sorting out the causes of civil war is difficult: historians cannot even agree on what caused the First World War. Most wars have multiple layers of causality: personalities, hatreds, mistakes. Our approach was to try to explain civil war statistically, looking at a range of possible causes: social, political, geographic, and economic.

The first and most critical step in statistical research is getting satisfactory data. We found a comprehensive list of civil wars produced at the University of Michigan, for many years the world's leading center for data on such political questions. The Michigan definition of civil war is an internal conflict that involves at least 1,000 combat-related deaths, with each side incurring at least 5 percent of these deaths. (One advantage of using criteria devised by another researcher is that your results cannot be contaminated by the temptation to bend definitions so as to get the results that you expect.) While the figure of 1,000 combat deaths is arbitrary, the point of drawing a line is that there really is a big difference between low-level communal violence in which, say, fifty people are killed and a war in which thousands get killed. We then matched this list of civil wars against a mass of socioeconomic data, country by country and year by year, with the goal of trying to determine the factors that affected the likelihood of a civil war developing in a given country within the next five years.

Our work has proved controversial. In part this is because the people attracted to the academic study of conflict tend to be politically engaged and are sympathetic to the acute grievances enunciated by various rebel movements, who often adopt extreme measures to oppose governments that indeed may be unsavory. To such academics, the whole idea of investigating statistically whether there is a relationship between objective measures of grievance and a propensity to rebel is taken to be more or less an insult, since they *know* there is one. Admittedly, we fanned the flames on occasion: we entitled one of our papers "Greed and Grievance" and another "Doing Well out of War," implying that rebel motivations may just conceivably not be any more heroic than the governments they oppose. At the less politicized end of the academic profession, however, our work has been taken seriously and frequently cited. We reached the policy world—I was invited to address the General Assembly of the United Nations—and have been featured in the media.

We were also asked to use our model to predict where the next civil wars would be—the CIA was apparently interested. But we were never that foolish. Our predictions might have been used as labels and thus likely to damage the very countries I was concerned to help; they might even have become self-fulfilling prophecies. More fundamentally, our model cannot be used for prediction. It *can* tell you what typically are the structural factors underlying proneness to civil war and—what is sometimes more interesting—what seems not to be very important. From this, it can tell you the sort of countries that are most at risk. But it cannot tell you whether Sierra Leone will have another civil war next year. That depends upon a myriad of short-term events.

The first link we found was between risk of war and initial level of income. Civil war is much more likely to break out in low-income countries: halve the starting income of the country and you double the risk of civil war. One might ask whether we got the causality mixed up—is it just that war makes a country poor, rather than that poverty makes a country prone to war? In fact, both relationships hold simultaneously. While civil war reduces income, low income indeed heightens the risk of civil war. The clearest evidence for this arises because during colonialism many countries experienced decades of enforced peace; the near-simultaneous decolonization of many countries with very different income levels provided a natural experiment for the effect of income on civil war.

The relationship between low income and civil war may seem obvious—if you read the newspapers, you will see that the countries where there is conflict are far more likely to be poor—but not all theorists of civil war have based their work on empirical data. Some social scientists, particularly the most politically engaged, know what they want to see in civil war and duly see it.

What else makes a country prone to civil war? Well, slow growth, or worse, stagnation or decline. As an approximation, a typical low-income country faces a risk of civil war of about 14 percent in any five-year period. Each percentage point added to the growth rate knocks off a percentage point from this risk. So if a country grows at 3 percent, the risk is cut from 14 percent to 11 percent; if its economy declines at 3 percent, the risk increases to 16 percent. On this point too, one might ask whether we have the causality backward—might it be the case instead that it is the *anticipation* of civil war that causes decline? After all, when a civil war looks to be in the cards, investors flee, and the economy declines. It looks like decline causes war, but actually it's the anticipation of war that causes decline. This objection can be dealt with by looking at a factor that affects growth but has no direct connection to civil war, and seeing whether the subsequent effects make civil war more or less likely. In low-income countries rainfall shocks (too much or too little rain) affect economic growth, but they do not directly affect the risk of civil war—that is, prospective rebels do not say, "It's raining, let's call off the rebellion." The effects on growth of rainfall shocks are thus clean of any ambiguity: they are not caused by anticipation of civil war. Yet setbacks to growth caused by rainfall shocks make civil war much more likely.

So if low income and slow growth make a country prone to civil war, it is reasonable to want to know why. There could be many explanations. My guess is that it is at least in part because low income means poverty, and low growth means hopelessness. Young men, who are the recruits for rebel armies, come pretty cheap in an environment of hopeless poverty. Life itself is cheap, and joining a rebel movement gives these young men a small chance of riches. In 2002 a little gang of rebels in the Philippines managed to kidnap some foreign tourists. A French woman among the kidnapped later described how she wrote down their demands for transmission to the authorities. "What do you want me to write?" she asked. "A million dollars per tourist" was what they wanted. She wrote it down, then asked, "Anything else?" A long pause, then a political thought: "Sack the mayor of Jolo." The last demand: "Two divers' wristwatches." That was the list of "totally justified" grievances from that particular

rebel group. Kidnapping tourists was just an unfortunate necessity to secure social justice. Anyway, the United States refused to pay up for the
American hostage, but the European governments paid up, with Muammar Qaddafi of Libya as a go-between, and in short order there was a
surge of young men wanting to join the rebels. This sort of recruitment
to a rebellion is a bit like joining drug gangs in the United States. A now-
famous study of a Chicago drug gang found that young men were attracted into the gang and willing to work for practically nothing because
of the small chance of big money if they managed to climb up the hierarchy
of the gang.

On top of that, if the economy is weak, the state is also likely to be weak,
and so rebellion is not difficult. Rebel leader Laurent Kabila, marching
across Zaire with his troops to seize the state, told a journalist that in Zaire,
rebellion was easy: all you needed was $10,000 and a satellite phone.
While this was obviously poetic exaggeration, he went on to explain that in
Zaire, everyone was so poor that with $10,000 you could hire yourself a
small army. And the satellite phone? Well, that takes us to the third and final economic risk factor in civil war: natural resources.

Dependence upon primary commodity exports—oil, diamonds, and
the like—substantially increases the risk of civil war. That's why Kabila
needed a satellite phone: in order to strike deals with resource extraction
companies. By the time he reached Kinshasa he reportedly had arranged
$500 million worth of deals. There have been several cases where interna-
tional companies have advanced massive amounts of funding to rebel
movements in return for resource concessions in the event of rebel victory.
That is apparently how Denis Sassou-Nguesso, the present president of
the Republic of the Congo (not to be confused with the Democratic Republic of the Congo, formerly Zaire), came to power. So natural resources
help to finance conflict and sometimes even help to motivate it. One example is "conflict diamonds." The UN defines them as "diamonds that origi-
nate from areas controlled by forces or factions opposed to legitimate and
internationally recognized governments, and are used to fund military action in opposition to those governments." In the case of conflict diamonds,
the attention that has been drawn to the problem by the NGO Global Wit-
ness has paid off. After years of denying that there was a problem, De
Beers, the world's largest diamond producer, has made amazing changes

that have gone a long way toward addressing the problem and have turned the company into a corporate role model.

So low income, slow growth, and primary commodity dependence make a country prone to civil war, but are they the *real* causes of civil war? I hear the phrase "root causes" a lot. It is bandied about at many of the conferences on conflict to which I am invited. Surprisingly frequently, a hypothesized root cause turns out to be predictable if you already know the hobbyhorse of the speaker. If the individual cares about income inequality, he or she imagines that that is what rebels are concerned about; someone strongly engaged with political rights assumes that rebels are campaigners for democracy; if someone's great-grandparents emigrated to escape from some oppressive regime, the person imagines that the descendants of those who did not emigrate are still being oppressed in the way that folk memory tells them once happened. Partly in response, the rebel groups generate a discourse of grievance that feeds these concerns, in effect inviting fellow travelers to imagine themselves wearing bandoliers on the barricades. Unfortunately, you simply can't trust the rebel discourse of concern for social justice: what else do you expect them to say?

Donations from diasporic communities have been one of the key sources of finance for rebel movements, so rebels have learned how to manipulate their public relations. The Irish Republican Army (IRA) attracted money from Irish Americans, and not just money, either—apparently some of the guns used by the IRA came from the Boston police department (though the attacks of September 11, 2001, brought a stop to that one, once Americans realized what terrorism actually meant). The Tamil Tigers got money from Tamils in Canada; the bomb that killed or injured more than 1,400 people in Sri Lanka's capital city, Colombo, in 1996 was paid for from a Canadian bank account. Albanians across the European Union financed the Kosovo Liberation Army, a group that some European politicians actually mistook for a decent political movement until it got its chance to murder. The best-organized diaspora movement of all was the Eritrean People's Liberation Front. The diaspora financed the war for thirty years, and in 1992 they won. Eritrea is now an independent country. But did the war really achieve a liberation of the Eritrean people? In September 2001, after an unnecessary international war with Ethiopia, half the Eritrean cabinet wrote to the president, Isaias Afwerki, asking him to think again about his autocratic style of government. He thought about it and imprisoned them all. He then instituted mass conscription of Eritrean youth. Ethiopia demobilized, but not Eritrea. Eritrean youth may be in the army as much to protect the president from protest as to protect the country from Ethiopia. Many young Eritreans have left the country. As I write, the government is in the process of expelling international peace observers, presumably so that it can restart the war. Was such a liberation really worth thirty years of civil war? As a side effect, it cut Ethiopia off from access to the sea. (Wait until Chapter 4 to see what that does.)

You might be ready to accept that rebel movements are good at public relations and use grievance as a weapon, but surely, you think, their underlying grievances must be well founded. Sometimes they are, because governments can be truly terrible. But is it generally true that well-founded grievances provoke rebellion? The evidence is much weaker than you might imagine. Take the repression of political rights. Political scientists have measured this sort of behavior, scoring it year by year, government by government. There is basically no relationship between political repression and the risk of civil war. Take economic or political discrimination against an ethnic minority. Two political scientists at Stanford, Jim Fearon and David Laitin, have measured this for more than two hundred ethnic minorities around the world. They found no relationship between whether a group was politically repressed and the risk of civil war. Ethnic minorities are just as likely to rebel with or without discrimination. Fearon and Laitin did the same for intergroup hatreds and again found no relationship to the risk of civil war. Anke Hoeffler and I investigated the effect of income inequality, and to our surprise we could find no relationship. We also investigated the colonial history of each country. We could find no relationship between the subsequent risk of civil war and either the country that had been the colonial power or how long the country had been decolonized. I even came to doubt the apparently incontestable notion that today's conflicts are rooted in history. Of course, pretty well wherever you find a conflict today it's true that there was a conflict in the same area some time in the remote past; the current participants usually make a lot of it, and a rebel leader can often get trouble going by appealing to the past. This does not mean that the past conflict caused the present one, however, nor that we are locked into conflict by history. Most of the places that are at peace now have had civil wars some time in the past. Rather, some economic conditions lend themselves to being taken advantage of by gutter politicians who build their success on hatred.

I do not want to push this too far, and I certainly do not want to condone governments that perpetrate discrimination or repression. Genuine grievances should be redressed whether or not they provoke rebellion, yet all too often they are not redressed. But the sad reality seems to be that grievances are pretty common. Rebels usually have something to complain about, and if they don't they make it up. All too often the really disadvantaged are in no position to rebel; they just suffer quietly. Looking through history, about the worst case of ethnic discrimination I can think of occurred after the Norman invasion of England. The Normans, a small group of violent, French-speaking Vikings, killed the English elite, stole all the land, and subjected the native 98 percent of the population to two centuries of servitude. During this time there were many civil wars. None of them was a rebellion of English serfs against Norman masters. All the civil wars were one bunch of Norman barons against another, trying to grab yet more resources.

A flagrant grievance is to a rebel movement what an image is to a business. But occasionally we can disentangle a rebellion enough to get past the image. In Fiji, for example, Indian immigration changed the balance of the population, and eventually the better-educated and richer Indians became a small majority; in 1999 they elected an ethnic Indian prime minister, Mahendra Chaudhry. Fiji is the world's foremost exporter of mahogany, and shortly after the Chaudhry government came to power it decided to put out the state mahogany plantations to international management. Two of the international bidders were the Commonwealth Development Corporation, a British not-for-profit organization with huge experience working in developing countries, and a private U.S. company. As is normal, each of these rival bidders hired local businessmen to support their bids, and in an atmosphere of intense competition the government awarded the contract to the Commonwealth Development Corporation. One month later, a indigenous Fijian rebel leader named George Speight—who also happened to be the same businessman who had been serving as a consultant to the U.S. company—began an armed struggle against the new government. Speight's slogan, "Fiji for the Fijians," was a very emotive rallying cry, but was social justice really Speight's only motive? I suppose that as a rallying cry "Give the mahogany contract to the Americans" would have lacked some of the same frisson of an implied struggle on behalf of the oppressed.

How about Sierra Leone? Sierra Leone is a poor and miserable country at the bottom of the Human Development Index (a composite measure of life expectancy, literacy, and income), and its inhabitants most surely have plenty of reasons for grievance. The rebel leader Foday Sankoh came close to hitting the jackpot of gaining power—his forces were so strong relative to those of the government that he was offered amazingly generous settlement terms, including the post of vice president. Remarkably, Sankoh turned it down; having the number two position in the country was not what he wanted. Instead, he made it very clear that his goal was to be in charge of the part of the government that managed Sierra Leone's lucrative diamond concessions. And Sankoh's rebellion had not exactly been the stuff of heroic armed struggle. His preferred recruits were teenage drug addicts, easily controlled and not excessively inhibited by moral scruples. Their favored strategy was terror against the civilian population, including hacking off the hands and feet of villagers, even children.

Let's move on to another illusion: that all civil war is based in ethnic strife. This may seem self-evident if you go by newspaper accounts, but I have come to doubt it. Most societies that are at peace have more than one ethnic group. And one of the few low-income countries that is completely ethnically pure, Somalia, had a bloody civil war followed by complete and persistent governmental meltdown. Statistically, there is not much evidence of a relationship between ethnic diversity and proneness to civil war. We do find some effect: societies that have one group that is large enough to form a majority of the population, but where other groups are still significant—what we call "ethnic dominance"—are indeed more at risk. Examples are Rwanda and Burundi, which endured massively bloody conflict between Hutus and Tutsis, and also Iraq, where the country is divided among Sunnis, Shiites, and Kurds. Perhaps the majority group in such places throws its weight around, or perhaps the minority groups know that they cannot trust majority rule to protect them and so try to preempt domination by the majority with their own domination. But this effect is not huge, and most of the societies that make up the bottom billion are too diverse for any one group to be this dominant. People from different ethnic groups may not like each other, and there may be a noisy discourse of mutual accusation. But there is a big gap between interethnic dislike and civil war.

What else makes a country prone to civil war? Geography matters a bit. A huge country with the population dispersed around the edges, such as the Democratic Republic of Congo (formerly Zaire), or one with a lot of mountainous terrain, such as Nepal, is more at risk than flat, densely populated little places, probably because rebel armies find more places to form and to hide.

Why Do Civil Wars Last So Long?

So much for the causes of civil war. What happens once a civil war has started? The most important question seems to be what determines when the conflict stops, yet it is not always easy to figure this out; often such conflicts stop temporarily and then start up again later. Is such a case to be treated as if there was one continuous civil war or two wars with an aborted peace in between? There is no right answer; it is a matter of judgment, and these judgments will affect the results. Again, we used others' criteria, to avoid having our own biases influence the data.

Once more, low income featured. The lower a country's income at the onset of a conflict, the longer the conflict lasts. There was also some tendency for wars to last longer if important export products of the society became more valuable; perhaps in such cases war becomes easier to finance. The ultimate natural resource war was in Angola, with the rebel group, the National Union for the Total Independence of Angola (UNITA), financed by diamonds, and the government side, the Popular Movement for the Liberation of Angola (MPLA), financed by oil. The course of the war broadly followed the price of oil relative to diamonds. The UNITA leader, Jonas Savimbi, intensified the pressure when he had a high income from diamonds and oil prices were at record lows. His undoing began when the price of oil rocketed and when international action started to close off his access to the world diamond market. But that story of international action must wait for Part 4.

Civil wars are highly persistent. The average international war, which is nasty enough, lasts about six months. You can do a lot of damage in six months. But the average civil war lasts more than ten times as long, even longer if you start off poor. In part, such conflicts continue because they become normal. On both sides interests develop that only know how to do well during war. Given the massive costs of war, it should be possible to find a deal that benefits everyone, but often the rebels decide to continue the struggle rather than take the risk of being lured into a peace deal on which the government subsequently reneges.

Having looked at why civil wars started and how long they lasted, we then looked at what happened when they were over. As previously noted, the end of a war often is not the end of the conflict; once over, a conflict is alarmingly likely to restart. Furthermore, the experience of having been through a civil war roughly doubles the risk of another conflict. Only around half of the countries in which a conflict has ended manage to make it through a decade without relapsing into war. Low-income countries face disproportionately high risks of relapse.

Governments in postconflict societies are well aware that they are living dangerously. Typically, they react to this risk by maintaining their military spending at an abnormally high level. The military during the postconflict decade looks much more like a military at war than one at peace. To give you the orders of magnitude, a civil war typically comes close to doubling the military budget. Military spending during the postconflict decade is only around a tenth lower than during the war. You can hardly blame governments that face such a high risk of further conflict for setting spending at such a high level, but does it work? I will come back to that in Part 4, which addresses possible solutions, and in particular Chapter 9, which discusses military strategies for keeping the peace.

The Costs of War

Finally, we looked at what you might think of as the balance sheet of a civil war: the costs and the legacy. Civil war is development in reverse. It damages both the country itself and its neighbors. Let's start with the country itself. Civil war tends to reduce growth by around 2.3 percent per year, so the typical seven-year war leaves a country around 15 percent poorer than it would have been. Of course, war is much worse than just a prolonged economic depression: it kills people. Overwhelmingly, the people who die are not killed in active combat but succumb to disease. Wars create refugees, and mass movements of the population in the context of collapsing public health systems create epidemics. A young Spanish researcher, Marta Reynol-Querol, analyzed civil war, migration movements, and the incidence of malaria and came up with a startling result: the migration triggered by civil war sharply increases the incidence of disease among the population in the havens to which refugees run. The increase is too large simply to be accounted for by the refugees themselves; what seems to happen is that in their trek across country, refugees are exposed to disease vectors to which they have little resistance, and the diseases they pick up then move with them to their place of refuge, also infecting the people already living in that area.

Both economic losses and disease are highly persistent: they do not stop once the fighting stops. Most of the costs of civil war, perhaps as much as half, accrue after the war is over. Of course, sometimes the rebellion is worth it, with rebel victory ushering in an age of social justice, but this does not happen often. Usually the political legacy is about as bad as the economic legacy—a deterioration in political rights. A rebellion is an extremely unreliable way of bringing about positive change. Rebel leaders who claim to have launched a civil war for the good of their country are usually deceiving themselves, others, or both. By the early 1990s, for example, Jonas Savimbi had amassed a fortune estimated at around $4 billion from UNITA's control of Angolan diamonds. After losing the presidential election he spent it selflessly on relaunching the civil war rather than on a billionaire lifestyle.

Their followers, the foot soldiers of rebellion, often do not have much choice about joining the rebel movement. I have previously noted Foday Sankoh's preference for recruiting teenage drug addicts. In Uganda the Lord's Resistance Army, whose stated goal is to establish government according to the Ten Commandments, recruits members by surrounding a remote school with troops and setting fire to the school. The boys who manage to run out are given the choice of being shot or joining up. Those who join are then required to commit an atrocity in their home district, such as raping an old woman, which makes it harder for the boys to go back home. This style of recruitment is less exceptional than you might think. When the Maoist rebel group in Nepal moves into a district the young men run away rather than join up: apparently, they fear the same sort of forced recruitment. And, looking back, it now turns out that recruitment for the Long March of the Chinese revolution, the stuff of revolutionary legend for two generations of Western romantics, was at the point of a gun. The soldiers were not ideologically committed revolutionaries but scared farmers. And during the Russian Revolution the government rapidly collapsed, effectively leaving both the Red Army and the White Army as rebels living off the land; four million men deserted, despite harsh treatment of any who were caught in the attempt. Interestingly, the desertion rate varied: it was much higher in summer, despite the harsh Russian winter. Why? The recruits were peasant farmers, and in the summer, when they had crops to attend to, fighting was just too costly for them, whereas in the winter it didn't matter so much. Economic opportunities really do shape the ease with which a rebel army can maintain its forces.

Scholars are now starting to study the rebel recruitment process more rigorously, through fieldwork among rebels. Jeremy Weinstein, a young professor at Stanford, has been working on a former rebel group, the Mozambican National Resistance (RENAMO), and the Revolutionary United Front (RUF), a particularly violent group in Sierra Leone. One of Jeremy's results is both important and depressing: it concerns the gradual erosion of initial motivations among a rebel group. Imagine that you are a rebel leader who has decided to build a movement to fight for social justice. You have bought some guns, or been given them by a friendly foreign government that wants to cause trouble, and now you need recruits. Young men turn up at your bush headquarters and volunteer. Should you accept them? Some of these volunteers are like you, potential warriors for social justice, but others are, unfortunately, just attracted by the opportunity to strut around with a gun. Too, according to psychologists, on average about 3 percent of any population have psychopathic tendencies, so you can be sure that some of those in the recruitment line will be psychopaths. Others will be attracted by the prospect of power and riches, however unlikely; if the reality of daily existence is otherwise awful, the chances of success do not have to be very high to be alluring. Even a small chance of the good life as a successful rebel becomes worth taking, despite the high risk of death, because the prospect of death is not so much worse than the prospect of life in poverty. The key point of Weinstein's research is that in the presence of natural resource wealth—oil, diamonds, or perhaps drugs—there are credible prospects of riches, so that some of the young men in the queue to join will be motivated by these prospects rather than by the mission to deliver social justice. The idealistic rebel leader will find it very difficult to screen these people out. He can try rejecting those who fail to come up with the right slogans. But soon everyone will learn to parrot them. Gradually, the composition of the rebel group will shift from idealists to opportunists and sadists.

One important incipient rebellion is taking place in the delta region of Nigeria, where the country's oil comes from. Aderoju Oyefusi, a Nigerian doctoral student, has recently done a survey of 1,500 people from the region to find out who is taking part. The delta region is the stuff of rebel legend because it combines four toxic ingredients: oil companies (greed), degradation of the environment (sacrilege), government military intervention (oppression), and a dead hero, the activist Ken Saro-Wiwa, who was hanged by the Nigerian government in 1995 (sanctity). Aderoju wanted to determine whether local people who joined the violent groups were those who were most aware of grievances. He measured this by asking people whether they felt a sense of grievance and classifying them accordingly. Astonishingly, he found that people with a sense of grievance were no more likely to take part in violent protest than those who were not aggrieved. So what characteristics did make people more likely to engage in political violence? Well, the three big ones were being young, being uneducated, and being without dependents. Try as one might, it is difficult to reconcile these characteristics of recruitment with an image of a vanguard of fighters for social justice.

And where are the violent groups most likely to form? One might think it would be in the districts that are most deprived of social amenities, for that is supposedly what it is all about—oil wealth being stolen by the oil companies and the federal government instead of being used for the benefit of local communities. But Aderoju found that among these 1,500 people there was no relationship between the social amenities that a district possessed and its propensity to political violence. Instead, the violence occurred in the districts with oil wells. The natural inference from this, given the prevailing discourse, is that this demonstrates that the oil companies are to blame because of all that environmental damage. But if this is indeed the explanation, we hit a further puzzle, because although the risk of violence jumps sharply if there is at least one oil well, if there are two oil wells in the district it starts to go down again. And with twenty oil wells it is lower still. That is odd because the environmental damage is presumably roughly proportional to the number of oil wells. To my mind this looks more like a story of a protection racket than outrage provoked by environmental damage. In the absence of an oil well there is no scope for extortion, and so no violent protest. With an oil well, the protection racket is in business. But the more oil wells there are in the district the greater the incentive for the oil company to pay up and buy peace.

I do not want to overstate these results, for the disputes in the delta started out as justified environmental protests by people living in a region that was bearing the brunt of damage without seeing the benefits of oil revenues. But over time the situation has evolved. There is now a huge amount of money being directed by the Nigerian federal government to the delta region, and the oil companies are desperately spreading protection money—paying ransoms to free kidnapped workers is pretty well a daily occurrence. Within the region local politicians are fighting it out for control of all this money, and violent protest has become an orchestrated part of this political rent seeking. Grievance has evolved, over the course of a decade, into greed.

Let us get back to the costs of conflict. Many of the costs are borne by neighboring countries. Diseases don't respect frontiers, and the economic collapse also spreads. Since most countries are bordered by several others, the overall cost to neighbors can easily exceed the cost to the country itself. And the costs are not limited to the immediate geographic region. Ninety-five percent of global production of hard drugs, for example, is from conflict countries. There is a straightforward explanation: conflict generates territory outside the control of a recognized government, and this comes in handy if your activity is illegal. Osama bin Laden chose to locate in Afghanistan for the same reason. So countries in civil war have what might be called a comparative advantage in international crime and terrorism. AIDS probably spread through an African civil war: the combination of mass rape and mass migration produces ideal conditions for spreading sexually transmitted disease. Consequently, wars in the bottom billion are our problem as well.

All in all, the cost of a typical civil war to the country and its neighbors can be put at around $64 billion. In recent decades about two new civil wars have started each year, so the global cost has been over $100 billion a year, or around double the global aid budget. This is obviously only a ballpark figure, although in building it we have erred on the side of caution. Nevertheless, this sort of cost estimate can be useful. It is a critical step in valuing the benefits of interventions. As you will see in Part 4, there is a range of interventions that can cut the risk of civil war. In any one instance it is impossible to value the benefits. However, using variants of our model, it is possible to work out how much, on average, a particular type of intervention will reduce the risk, and so reduce the global incidence of civil war. By combining this reduction in the incidence of war with our estimate of the cost of war we deduce a benefit for the intervention. Once this benefit is combined with the cost of the intervention, we have arrived at the cost-benefit analysis.

Cost-benefit analysis is the basis of how governments make decisions on public spending. If we can get interventions to reduce the risk of civil war into this conventional framework of public decision making, we can escape the world of political make-believe—the posturing fantasies to which politicians resort when unrestrained by evidence. That is ultimately the agenda of Part 4.

The Conflict Trap

Now we reach the aspect of civil war that is crucial for the thesis of this book: it is a trap. Suppose a country starts its independence with the three economic characteristics that globally make a country prone to civil war: low income, slow growth, and dependence upon primary commodity exports. It is playing Russian roulette. That is not just an idle metaphor: the risk that a country in the bottom billion falls into civil war in any five-year period is nearly one in six, the same risk facing a player of Russian roulette. The country may be lucky and grow its way out of the danger zone before it gets caught. Growth directly helps to reduce risk; cumulatively it raises the level of income, which also reduces risk, and that in turn helps to diversify the country's exports away from primary commodities, which further reduces risk. But it may not be so lucky. Suppose that for one reason or another growth stays slow. (I will be looking at why the countries of the bottom billion have failed to grow in the following chapters.) Then the peace might not last long enough to bring risks down before the chamber with the bullet in it comes around and the country slides into civil war. That is basically what has happened: the unlucky countries got war shortly after independence, as in the case of Nigeria, while others maintained peace for many years and then succumbed, as did Côte d'Ivoire, which was destabilized by a coup d'état, and Nepal, where Maoists were confronted by a fratricidal monarchy. All have been living dangerously. Sooner or later some combination of personalities and mistakes that in a more economically successful country would be brushed aside escalates into rebellion. Call the personalities and mistakes the "causes" if you must. I think that in such fragile societies it is generally even harder to avoid these triggers than it is to develop the economy. Persuading everyone to behave decently to each other because the society is so fragile is a worthy goal, but it may be more straightforward just to make the societies less fragile, which means developing their economies. How we can help these countries to do that is the agenda for Part 4.

Once a war has begun, the economic damage undoes the growth achieved during peace. Worse, even aside from this economic damage the risk of further war explodes upward. Civil war leaves a legacy of organized killing that is hard to live down. Violence and extortion have proved profitable for the perpetrators. Killing is the only way they know to earn a living. And what else to do with all those guns? Currently one of my graduate students, Phil Killicoat, is trying to collect data on the price of a Kalashnikov around the world year by year, the Kalashnikov being the weapon of choice for any self-respecting rebel. That is the sort of innovation in data that would make a real contribution to work on conflict. It is not an easy task, which is why until now nobody has done it, but he is resourceful. The emerging pattern seems to be that guns become cheap during conflict because so many get imported through official and semiofficial channels that a proportion of them leak onto the informal market. The legacy of conflict is cheap Kalashnikovs.

Anke Hoeffler and I looked to see what happens to the crime rate in postconflict societies. Crime is one of the phenomena that are very badly measured: countries differ massively in their definitions and in the degree of underreporting. For that reason we settled on the homicide rate as the proxy for violent crime in general. Homicide is the best-defined violent crime and it is also likely to be the best-reported. We found that political peace does not usher in social peace. The end of the political fighting ushers in a boom in homicides. Presumably, this is part of a wider surge in violent crime. Add in mutual distrust and recriminations over atrocities, and it is not surprising that the typical postconflict country has little better than a fifty-fifty chance of making it through the first decade in peace. Indeed, about half of all civil wars are postconflict relapses.

A country such as the Democratic Republic of the Congo (formerly Zaire) will need around half a century of peace at its present rate of growth simply to get back to the income level it had in 1960. Its chances of getting fifty continuous years of peace with its low income, slow growth, dependence upon primary commodities, and history of conflict are, unfortunately, not high. This country is likely to be stuck in a conflict trap no matter how many times it rebrands itself unless we do something about it.

Poverty, economic stagnation, dependence on primary commodities—do these characteristics sound familiar? Yes, they are endemic to the bottom billion. This does not mean that all such countries are in the conflict trap, but they are all prone to it. We have, in fact, the building blocks for a system. The risk of conflict differs according to economic characteristics, and the economic characteristics are affected by conflict. It is possible to set up this interaction as a model that predicts in a stylized fashion how the incidence of conflict is likely to evolve. I joined forces with Harvard Hegre, a young Norwegian political scientist, and we built one. The world, as modeled, starts in 1960 with three different groups of countries: rich, bottom billion, and developing. We then see how many countries fall into conflict. The predictions rest upon the risks generated by the analysis I had already done with Anke, as well as assumptions about growth performance that extrapolate from the past forty years of experience. We project the incidence of conflict through until 2020 and even, somewhat fancifully, to 2050. Rich countries have such a low risk of civil war that even over such a long period none gets into trouble. A few of the developing countries stumble into civil war, and those that do get derailed for a while—examples of these are countries such as Colombia and Lebanon, which are not part of the bottom billion but for one reason or another have been unlucky. The bulk of the countries that fall into civil war are from the bottom billion. Periodically they get back to peace, but often they fall back into conflict. The model is useless for telling us which countries will be in conflict, but its prediction as to how the global incidence of conflict evolves is depressing. By 2020 the world is much richer than today, and by 2050 it is fabulously richer: most countries are developed. But the incidence of civil war declines only modestly because most civil war is generated by the minority of countries in the bottom billion, and their growth is slow. Our model quantifies the grim implications of the failure of the growth process in the bottom billion, given the link between poverty, stagnation, and conflict.

Coups

Rebellion is not the only form of violent, illegitimate challenge to governments in the countries of the bottom billion. Many governments are more at threat from coups than from rebellions. You might have thought that coups had died out; your image of a coup is likely to involve a Latin American general from the 1960s. There is some justice to that image, as coups have largely gone out of fashion and outside the bottom billion they are now very rare. But among the bottom billion they are still depressingly common. As of December 2006 the latest successful one had occurred just two weeks earlier, in Fiji. Coups are not as disastrous as civil wars; to adapt the famous newspaper headline about an earthquake, this event might have been reported as "small coup in Fiji, not many dead." But they are not a very good way of changing a government. The political instability that they manifest is known to be detrimental to economic development. So what causes coups?

We drew upon the data of an American political scientist who had assiduously trawled through thousands of pages of newspaper reports to produce a comprehensive list of all the reported coup plots, failed coup attempts, and successful coups in Africa, and we also found data on all the successful coups in other parts of the world. We followed broadly the same approach that we had taken in understanding civil wars. I should add a caveat: whereas our civil war work is published and so has been subject to academic scrutiny, our work on coups is new and so far has been presented only at a few conferences. However, I am sufficiently confident in these results to describe them, and what we found certainly surprised us.

It turns out that countries are prone to coups for reasons pretty similar to those that make them prone to civil war. The two big risk factors are low income and low growth—exactly the same as civil war. In Africa, societies with one big ethnic group—what we have called "ethnic dominance"—are also more at risk, just as with civil war. And, again crucially for the thesis of this book, there is a coup trap, just as there is a civil war trap. Once a country has had a coup it is much more likely to have further coups. The big difference between coups and rebellions is that natural resources do not seem to matter. This may be because to mount a rebellion you need to find a sustainable source of funds for guns and troops, so profiting from natural resources helps to make rebellion financially feasible, whereas to mount a coup you don't need any financing whatsoever—the government has already paid for the army that you are going to use against it.

Because Africa is the epicenter of low income and slow growth, it has become the epicenter of coups. But, controlling for these risk factors, there is no "Africa effect." Africa does not have more coups because it is Africa; it has more coups because it is poor. That's also true of civil war: Africa became increasingly prone to civil war as its economic performance deteriorated, not because it was Africa. Some years ago I found that my neighbor at a conference was a former vice president of Ghana. He explained that he was delighted to have been invited to the conference: the invitation had actually prompted his release from prison. He had been imprisoned following a coup d'état, and so we talked about that. He told me how unprepared the government had been for the coup; it was totally unexpected. Surely not, I said; coups are pretty common. He explained why the government considered itself safe: "By the time we came to power there was nothing left to steal."

At the high levels of coup risk prevalent in Africa, governments are, unsurprisingly, scared of their own armies. In principle the army is there to defend the government. In practice it is often the biggest threat to the government. I will return to this in Chapter 9, on the military.

Why It Matters for G8 Policy

Wars and coups keep low-income countries from growing and hence keep them dependent upon exports of primary commodities. Because they stay poor, stagnant, and dependent upon primary commodities they are prone to wars and coups. Wars and coups feed on themselves in other ways that make history repeat itself.

The costs that these conditions generate are predominantly borne not by those who perpetrate them. The costs of war even spread beyond the war's temporal and geographic boundaries. As a result, they not only trap the countries that experience them, but make development more difficult in entire regions.

If wars and coups could readily be avoided by good domestic political design—democratic rights—then the responsibility for peace would be predominantly internal. That is, we might reasonably think that peace should be a struggle waged by citizens of the country itself, rather than something for us to become actively concerned about. But the evidence is against such internal solutions. Democratic rights, hard as they are for a people to establish, do not reduce the risk of civil war, and they do not reduce the risk of coups. When the growth process fails in a low-income society, it is exposed to risks that are hard to contain. I do not want to claim that only the economy matters, but without growth peace is considerably more difficult. And in the societies of the bottom billion the economy is stuck. So breaking the conflict trap and the coup trap are not tasks that these societies can readily accomplish by themselves.

CHAPTER 3

The Natural Resource Trap

CONFLICT IS NOT THE ONLY TRAP. A much more paradoxical trap has been the discovery of valuable natural resources in the context of poverty. You would hope that the discovery of natural resource wealth would be a catalyst to prosperity, and sometimes it is. But these are the exceptions. Sometimes resource wealth has contributed to the conflict trap. But even where the country stays at peace it typically fails to grow; indeed, the surplus from natural resource exports significantly reduces growth. Economists term the excess of revenues over all costs including normal profit margins "rent," and rents seem to be damaging. Over time, countries with large resource discoveries can end up poorer, with the lost growth more than offsetting the one-off gain in income provided by the rents.

Obviously if you have enough natural resources you can afford to forget about normal economic activity. The whole society can live as rentiers, that is, on unearned income from wealth. This is the situation in Saudi Arabia and Persian Gulf states such as Kuwait, which have enormous oil revenues. But these wealthy rentier states are rare. A much larger group of resource-rich countries have enough income from resources to take them to middle-income status, but not beyond. To fully develop they would need to harness the resource wealth for growth. This has proved difficult, and the normal pattern has been stagnation, or rather booms and busts around a pretty flat trend. This describes much of the Middle East and Russia. What I have to say about the problems of resource wealth is pertinent for this group of stagnant middle-income countries. However, my main concern is with a third group of resource-rich countries: those that are poor. Resources loom large in such economies because the economies are so small, but they do not even bring the society up to middle-income status. The societies of the bottom billion are disproportionately in this category of resource-rich poverty: about 29 percent of the people in the bottom billion live in countries in which resource wealth dominates the economy. Thus resource wealth is an important part of the story of the poverty of the bottom billion.

So why is resource wealth a problem?

Curses, Curses . . .

The "resource curse" has been known for some time. Thirty years ago economists came up with an explanation termed "Dutch disease," after the effects of North Sea gas on the Dutch economy; it goes like this. The resource exports cause the country's currency to rise in value against other currencies. This makes the country's other export activities uncompetitive. Yet these other activities might have been the best vehicles for technological progress. We are going to meet Dutch disease again when we look at the effects of aid, so it is worth understanding it.

Take a country that neither has natural resource exports nor receives aid. Its citizens want to buy imports, and the only way they can pay for them is through exports. Exporters generate foreign exchange, and importers buy the foreign exchange off them to purchase the imports. It is the need to pay for imports that makes exports valuable to the society that produces them. Now, along come natural resource exports (or aid, for that matter). The resources are sources of foreign exchange for the society. Exports lose their value domestically. Another way of saying the same thing is that items that cannot be traded internationally, such as local services and some foods, become more expensive and so resources get diverted into producing them. Take Nigeria in the 1970s. As oil revenues built up, the country's other exports—such as peanuts and cocoa—became unprofitable, and production rapidly collapsed. The loss of these agricultural activities hurt the farmers who had produced them, but it probably didn't of itself curtail the growth process because traditional export agriculture was generally not a very dynamic sector with many opportunities for technical progress and productivity growth. However, Dutch disease can damage the growth process by crowding out export activities that otherwise have the potential to grow rapidly. The key activities are labor-intensive manufactures and services, the sort of exporting now done by China and India. A low-income country with abundant natural resources is unlikely to be able to break into these markets because the foreign exchange they generate is not sufficiently valuable within the society.

Dutch disease is still an important idea in economics. As you will see, it is the basis of the latest critique of aid produced by the International Monetary Fund—the chief economist of the IMF thinks that aid is killing growth by killing exports. However, by the 1980s Dutch disease did not seem a sufficient explanation for the problems of resource-rich countries, so economists added concerns about shocks: natural resource revenues were volatile and this led to crises. This was the approach that I focused on when I first began my academic work in economics. I started with the Kenyan coffee boom of 1976–79 and went on to investigate other trade shocks around the world.

Volatile revenues are obviously difficult to manage. During a price boom government ministries, scenting the money available, put in outrageous bids for more spending. In Kenya one ministry raised its proposed budget thirteenfold and refused to prioritize. Probably it reckoned that other ministries were likely to do the same, so behaving responsibly was likely to leave it at the back of the line. With this sort of behavior, rational public investment is liable to go out the window. Worse, although public spending can be increased very rapidly during the boom phase, it proves very difficult to reduce during the subsequent crash. What gets cut is often not the frivolous items that went up during the boom, but whatever is politically the most vulnerable. So maybe employment in the diplomatic service goes up during the boom, whereas basic investment gets cut during the crash.

The boom-and-bust phenomenon also makes it very hard for electorates to sort out when a government is making mistakes. In the first half of the 1980s Nigeria enjoyed a huge oil boom. The government made a catastrophic mess of this boom, borrowing heavily and spending money on massively wasteful projects saturated with corruption. Yet inevitably, during the boom some of the good times trickled down to ordinary people. In 1986 the world price of oil crashed, and the Nigerian gravy train came to an abrupt end. Not only was oil revenue drastically reduced, but the banks were not willing to continue lending; they actually wanted to be paid back. The swing from big oil and borrowing to little oil and repayment approximately halved Nigerian living standards. Ordinary people were going to notice this catastrophic decline whether or not they understood why it was happening. At this point the government launched some limited economic reforms, with the much-trumpeted support of international financial institutions. The reforms were dressed up into a high-profile political package and called a structural adjustment program. Although the reforms were modest, they were remarkably successful: output grew more rapidly than at any time during the oil boom. But these few percentage points of growth in non-oil output were completely swamped by the fall in the value of oil and the switch from borrowing to repayment, with the consequent contraction in expenditure. The reform-induced growth only helped slightly to offset the misery of falling living standards. That is what happened, but it is not what Nigerians think happened. Unsurprisingly, Nigerians think that the terrible increase in poverty they experienced was caused by the economic reforms that were so loudly trumpeted. Until reform, life was getting better; then along came reform, and poverty soared. Given that belief, Nigerians go on to ask the obvious question: why did we undergo such devastating "reform"? The answer they arrive at, which is inescapable given the previous steps, is that the international financial institutions conspired to ruin Nigeria. Once when I visited Nigeria using the UN passport I then had, the initially beaming immigration officer caught sight of the words "World Bank" and his smile evaporated. "I'm not shaking *your* hand," he said. "The World Bank hates poor people." This understandable misreading of a boom-bust cycle has made it extremely hard to build a constituency for economic reform in Nigeria. Ordinary people—who would be the big beneficiaries of reform—long for the days of mismanagement because they were the days of boom. Marxists used to have a handy term for this sort of mass miscomprehension—false consciousness.

So volatility was what you would have learned about in the 1980s. By the mid-1990s there was more evidence to go on, and economist Jeffrey Sachs revived concern about the problem of natural resource rents. Since then political scientists have joined in, suggesting that resource revenues worsen governance. Without discounting the older economic explanations, I think the evidence points to governance as the key problem. However, I believe that the political scientists have not gone far enough in their analysis. They have generally seen the problem of resource rents as being proneness to autocracy: oil induces Saddam Hussein. There is good evidence for this, but the real problem is even worse.

The heart of the resource curse is that resource rents make democracy malfunction. You might think that democracy is precisely what resource-rich societies most need. After all, in such societies the state inevitably has lots of resources to manage, and democracy should provide some sort of discipline that dictators lack. That is, you might expect that democracy is at its most useful for the economy when there are lots of natural resources around. You might think so, but you would be wrong. I am going to propose a new law of the jungle of electoral competition in the presence of natural resources: *the survival of the fattest.*

Let's focus on oil, which is the big natural resource. Until recently, an oil democracy seemed almost an oxymoron. The Middle East, where oil supplies are concentrated, was uniformly autocratic, and this reflected a global pattern: oil rents have substantially reduced the likelihood that a society is democratic. Things are changing. Democracy is spreading to the oil economies, and oil is spreading to the low-income democracies. The spread of democracy to the oil economies is an explicit agenda—indeed, apparently the overarching agenda of the United States in the Middle East. In other regions democratization of important oil economies has occurred even without such explicit pressure, for example in Indonesia, Mexico, Nigeria, and Venezuela. The spread of oil to democracies is a side effect of the attempt to free U.S. oil supplies from dependence on the Middle East. New discoveries have been made in a range of low-income democracies, such as Gambia, São Tomé and Principe, Senegal, and East Timor.

There is quite a bit of institutional variation among resource-rich societies. Although institutions are affected by resource riches, usually countries got their institutions before they discovered their resources, hence the global variation in institutions is pretty well reflected among those with resource wealth. So it is possible to tease out statistically how political institutions interact with resource wealth.

Anke Hoeffler and I started by estimating the rents (that is, the excess of revenues over all costs) generated by natural resources, country by country and year by year. Estimating the rents on primary commodities is an important advance on just counting their value: the rent on $1 million of oil exports is much greater than the rent on $1 million of coffee exports because the costs of production are much lower. So data on primary commodity exports, which is what people had used when they had bothered to look at the numbers, are a poor guide to how valuable the resources really are. And even $1 million of oil exports generates a bigger surplus if it is coming from an easy-to-exploit onshore location than if it is deep offshore, and if the price per barrel is $60 rather than $10.

We then matched these surpluses with the political institutions of each country. Political scientists have classified the different gradations of democracy across the globe and over time, and we used this standard classification. We then tried to explain a country's growth over a given period in terms of the characteristics prevailing at the start of that period.

We found a consistent pattern, and it's not particularly good news for countries such as Iraq. Oil and other surpluses from natural resources are particularly unsuited to the pressures generated by electoral competition. Without natural resource surpluses, democracies outgrow autocracies. (This is itself quite an encouraging gloss on the economic consequences of democracy: the usual academic assessment is that democracy has no net effect on growth, and we think that is because studies have not controlled for natural resources.) In the presence of large surpluses from natural resources it is the other way around: autocracies outperform democracies, and the effects are large. In the absence of natural resource surpluses a fully democratic polity outperforms a despotic autocracy by around 2 percent per year. By the time natural resource rents are around 8 percent of national income, the growth advantage of democracy has been eliminated. Beyond this the net effect of democracy is adverse. Taking a country with resource rents worth 20 percent of national income, the switch from autocracy to intense electoral competition would lower the growth rate by nearly 3 percent.

Why does democracy undermine the ability to harness resource surpluses? One possibility is that resource surpluses induce an excessively large public sector—the opposite of the "minimal state" fashionable with conservatives during the 1980s. We tested this by controlling for the share of public expenditure in national income. But this does not reduce the adverse effect of democracy on the use of natural resource surpluses. The reason the resource-rich democracies underperform is not simply that governments spend too much. We then turned to the composition of expenditure—was the problem one of spending on the wrong things? The most basic influence on economic growth is investment. Once we controlled for the share of investment, the remaining adverse effect of democracy became smaller. This suggests that the resource-rich democracies underinvest. In fact, this is no surprise. Other researchers have found that quite generally democracies tend to underinvest: governments are so fixated on winning the next election that they disregard what might happen afterward, and so neglect investments that only come to fruition in the future. In resource-rich societies investment is evidently particularly important since this is how the resource surplus can be transformed into sustained increases in income; underinvesting becomes an even more important mistake. However, the main story turns out to be not the *rate* of investment but the *return* on investment. The resource-rich democracies not only underinvest but invest badly, with too many white-elephant projects.

Why Do Resource Surpluses Mess Up Politics?

To see how democratic politics goes wrong in the context of resource riches, the concept of democracy has to be unbundled into its component parts. Democracy is not just about elections. Some of the rules of democracy do indeed determine how power is *achieved,* and that's where elections come in. But other rules of democracy limit how power is *used.* These rules are concerned with checks and balances on government abuse of power. Both sets of rules get undermined by resource rents.

An abundance of resource rents alters how electoral competition is conducted. Essentially, it lets in the politics of patronage. Electoral competition forces political parties to attract votes in the most cost-effective manner. In normal circumstances this is done by delivering public services such as infrastructure and security more effectively than rivals can. The extreme alternative to public service politics is the politics of patronage: voters are bribed with public money. One of the reasons for secret ballots was to prevent bribery. But in some societies there are ways around secret ballots—for example, a party can start a rumor that the ballot is not really secret, or it can buy registration cards off the supporters of other candidates so that they cannot vote. The tragedy is that where bribery becomes acceptable it can be effective, because using your vote to support a party offering public services rather than selling it to the patronage party is not in your individual self-interest. Why not sell your own vote and leave it to others to vote in the national interest? Patronage starts to look cost-effective for a political party if votes can be bought wholesale by bribing a few opinion leaders; from the perspective of a cynical politician, the very universality of public services starts to look wasteful. Just as it is rational for fashion companies to focus their marketing efforts on opinion leaders, so it is rational for a political party that is going to buy its votes through patronage to concentrate its money on buying community leaders. Voting in blocs at the behest of such leaders is most likely where voter loyalty to ethnic communities is strong and where the objective information available to the typical voter is weak. These are, unfortunately, typical in the societies of the bottom billion. Indeed, we found that the more ethnically diverse the society, the worse the performance of a resource-rich democracy. Similarly, the less free the press, the worse democracy's performance in resource-rich countries.

Suppose, then, we accept that in the context of ethnic loyalties and the absence of press freedom, patronage politics is more cost-effective than the provision of public services as a strategy for winning elections. This still leaves open the question as to why it is disproportionately a problem in resource-rich societies. After all, many societies have ethnic diversity and limited freedom of the press.

In many societies patronage politics might be a more cost-effective use of public money to attract votes than the provision of public services, yet it is too expensive to be feasible. For this strategy to be feasible, the ruling political party has to be able to subvert public funds. Obviously, a key difference between using resource revenues to supply public services and using them to supply private patronage is that patronage breaks all the rules of how public resources should be managed. To finance patronage the government first needs to embezzle public money out of the budget and into slush funds. If the restraints upon embezzlement are sufficiently tight, then patronage politics is simply too expensive to be feasible. This, we believe, is where resource rents play such a subversive role. If there are effective checks and balances on power, the society is saved from patronage politics even though, were they given the chance, political parties would be driven by electoral competition to play that game. Happily for societies with effective checks and balances, this is reinforced by the selection of politicians according to their intrinsic motivation to serve the public. Where patronage politics is not feasible, the people attracted to politics are more likely to be interested in issues of public services provision. Of course, for the societies where patronage is feasible, this works in reverse: democratic politics then tends to attract crooks rather than altruists. Economists generally think that competition produces the survival of the fittest. But where patronage politics is feasible, electoral competition leaves the corrupt as the winners. And so we arrive at the law of the political jungle: the survival of the fattest.

The head of the Nigerian tax authority invited me out one evening. In fact, he was the ex-head, having just resigned to go back to the private sector, from where he had been recruited. Over dinner he told me why he could not take any more. For two years he had been trying to get a small piece of tax legislation through the legislature: it was not contentious, just a technical cleanup operation. Its passage depended upon the chair of the relevant committee—who had said to him, "How much?" That is, the chair of the committee had expected to be bribed by the tax authority. No bribe, no law. Why? Because that was normal; that was how it was done. Cumulatively, patronage politics had attracted crooks.

Why do big resource revenues weaken political restraints? One reason is obvious: they radically reduce the need to tax. Because resource-rich countries do not need to tax, they do not provoke citizens into supplying the public good of scrutiny over how their taxes are being spent. While in its general form this undermining of accountability has been understood for a long time, it has usually been seen as an explanation of why resource-rich societies are more likely to be autocratic. Our key point is that this same undermining of accountability operates within polities that, at least on the criterion of electoral competition, are democratic. What gets undermined is not electoral competition but the political restraints on how power is used.

We found that resource rents gradually erode checks and balances. This leaves electoral competition unconstrained by the niceties of due process. Political parties are freed up to compete for votes by means of patronage if they so choose, and in the context of ethnic loyalties and the absence of a free press, this is the most cost-effective means of attracting votes. Any quixotic parties that choose the public service route of appealing to voters simply lose the election.

Political scientists have developed a quantitative measure of political restraints on power. As with all quantification, the system has its deficiencies: it simply adds up how many of seventeen possible checks and balances are incorporated into a political system—an independent judiciary, an independent press, and suchlike. It is not ideal, but it is better than nothing. Some democracies are long on electoral competition and short on checks and balances, some are the other way around, and the mature democracies of developed countries generally have both. When we introduced both measures into our explanation of growth, we found that they interacted with resource rents in precisely opposite ways. Whereas electoral competition significantly worsened the contribution of resource rents to growth, restraints significantly improved it.

With sufficiently powerful restraints a resource-rich democracy can be an economic success. What does "sufficient" mean in practice? Let's return to that example of a country with resource rents worth 20 percent of GDP and with intense electoral competition. Remember that in the absence of checks and balances the society was losing nearly three percentage points off the growth rate compared with an autocracy. On the quantitative scale of checks and balances that we use, the society would need only four of the seventeen possible restraints in order to eliminate this disadvantage, and with eight restraints it would be outperforming the autocracy by 2.8 percentage points. Four restraints out of seventeen do not sound like that many, but unfortunately that is double what the resource-rich societies typically have. The resource-rich countries are more in need of checks and balances than other countries, but paradoxically have fewer of them.

If a society just added any four of the seventeen restraints, would it be enough to do the trick? Most likely not. The quantitative index is just a crude approximation, not a blueprint. It does not tell us which checks and balances matter most, nor how they interact, nor how they are affected by cultural context. We have pretty well reached the limits of what we are able to tease out of quantitative research. We were, however, able to probe just a little further. If any restraint is important, it is surely a free press. An organization called Freedom House has, over the years, put together a global scoring system of press freedom. The scoring is pretty rough: free, partially free, not at all free. We used it to investigate whether press freedom mattered differentially in resource-rich societies. We found that a free press was quite generally associated with a faster growth rate, but that the effect was significantly larger in the context of resource riches.

Finally, we tried to track down which policies were improved by restraints. As far as we can tell, it comes back to the investment decision: restraints raise the return on investment. One practical illustration of how checks and balances can work to raise the returns on investment can be seen in Nigeria, Africa's most important oil-rich country. For over a decade prior to 1979 Nigeria had been run by military dictators. To general relief, in that year the country returned to democratic civilian rule, electing Shehu Shagari president. Unfortunately, his regime turned out to be a classic example of patronage-driven electoral competition unrestrained by checks and balances. One of the government's first acts was to recall a massive public investment project for a dam that had been awarded under the military government. The project was reawarded, but its cost according to the new contract rose from $120 million to an amazing $600 million. Politicians had spent a fortune buying the votes that got them elected, and now needed urgently to recoup their investments; their means to do so was to profit from the dam project.

A second example, also from Nigeria, is much more recent. At the end of 1983 Nigeria plunged back into military dictatorship, returning to civilian democratic rule again in 1998. By 2003 Olusegun Obasanjo was starting his second elected term as president (he had also been head of state under military rule from 1976 to 1979). His first elected term had, like the Shagari regime, been a transition from military rule to democracy and had indeed been a rerun of that regime. Electoral competition was intense: in the 2003 elections 80 percent of incumbent senators had been defeated. By contrast, checks and balances were virtually nonexistent: there had been no time to put them in place, and all the powerful sectional interests were opposed to them. With considerable courage, at the start of his second term President Obasanjo began to introduce the missing checks and balances. One of the first restraints, astonishing only in that it had previously been absent, was to require that public investment projects be put out for competitive bidding. When this requirement was first introduced it was made slightly retroactive: some projects that had previously been approved were recalled. The process of competitive bidding reduced the cost of these recalled projects by an average of 40 percent.

These two Nigerian examples—the massive increase in the cost of a dam generated by the transition to unrestrained electoral competition, and the massive reduction in costs generated by basic restraints—illustrate the sheer scale of the dangers facing the resource-rich democracies.

So Is It Back to Autocracy?

The rather depressing evidence gathered above might appear to suggest that the resource-rich societies should stick with autocracy. That would be a pretty distasteful result—after all, democracy is desirable for powerful reasons irrespective of its effect on the economy. However, for nearly all the societies of the bottom billion, autocracy would also be wrong even in economic terms. There is a powerful reason why autocracy does not work well in most societies of the bottom billion: ethnic diversity.

I have already discussed ethnic diversity in the context of the conflict trap. There I was able to be quite upbeat: there is little link between ethnic diversity and an elevated risk of conflict. But its wider effects on the economic growth process are less benign. Autocracy seems to work well for the economy only in societies that are not ethnically diverse. The astonishing success of China glows like a beacon to some of the autocrats of bottom-billion societies, but it is a radically misleading comparison. China is an example of a homogeneous autocracy, whereas many bottom-billion societies are characterized by ethnically diverse autocracies. Globally, autocracy in ethnically diverse societies reduces growth, and the most likely reason is that diversity tends to narrow the support base of the autocrat. Typically, in ethnically diverse societies autocrats depend upon the support of their own ethnic group—think of Saddam Hussein, who was a Sunni Muslim and whose Baath Party was composed mainly of Sunnis, to the detriment of Iraq's Shiites and Kurds. The more diverse the society, the smaller the autocrat's group is likely to be. This in turn changes the incentives for the autocrat. The narrower the base of social support, the stronger the incentive for economic policy to sacrifice growth in order to redistribute income to the autocrat's group.

Hence, in the context of ethnic diversity such as in Nigeria, and indeed Iraq, autocracy has failed to generate conditions conducive to growth, and its return would hold no promise of improvement. The uncomfortable implication is that electoral competition is not enough to overcome the blockage to growth generated by autocracy; it merely shifts the form of the blockage to a more broadly diffused wastage of resources through patronage. In the context of ethnic diversity and resource rents, electoral competition is necessary but not sufficient.

The resource-rich, ethnically diverse societies need a democracy that is distinctive in having a strong emphasis on political restraints relative to electoral competition. This cocktail is rare, but it does exist. An example is Botswana, a country rich in diamonds. Although Botswana has been a democracy continuously since its independence, none of its elections has actually changed the government; electoral competition could not reasonably be described as intense. It has, however, managed to preserve adherence to due process. A notable aspect of this has been that all public investment projects have been required to meet a minimum rate of return. The clear evidence that this has been enforced is that a very large amount of surplus funds has been accumulated in foreign assets. Democracy in Botswana thus stands in contrast to past democracy in Nigeria: the two have had a radically different balance between electoral competition and checks and balances. They have also had radically different growth outcomes: Botswana has transformed itself into a middle-income country, decisively escaping the bottom billion. Indeed, for a long period it achieved the world's fastest growth rate.

Why Is Natural Resource Abundance a Trap?

Why do I describe natural resource abundance in the societies of the bottom billion as a trap? Oil has been fine for Norway, so why not for Chad? I do not want to underplay the conventional economic explanations: Dutch disease and volatility in commodity prices. They inhibit growth even if a country's politics are reasonable. Between them they come close to closing off a country's chances of diversifying into manufactured and service exports, and these are pretty big opportunities to close off. And I think that the political science explanation is also important: resource rents are likely to induce autocracy. In the ethnically diverse societies of the bottom billion such autocracies are likely to be highly detrimental for economic development, as was Saddam Hussein's rule in Iraq. But what I have been concerned to show is that even replacing autocracy with democracy—not an easy thing to do, since autocrats generally cling tenaciously to power— is unlikely to be enough. The sort of democracy that the resource-rich societies of the bottom billion are likely to get is itself dysfunctional for economic development. In the transition to democracy there are strong incentives for different groups to compete for election, but there are no corresponding incentives for them to build restraints. Restraints are a public good that it is in nobody's particular interest to supply.

So if resource riches are so bad for restraints, how come Norway has them? Well, it got them before it got its oil. Not only is growth good in itself, but it feeds back upon the rules of the political game. Political restraints are promoted by a higher level of per capita income. Economic development gradually induces healthy institutional change. So political institutions in part reflect past growth as well as influence future growth. Norway has nothing special by way of restraints—it just has the sort of rules that are normal for its level of development.

It is this that creates the possibility of a political development trap. A low-income, resource-rich society that either is an ethnically diverse autocracy or acquires the instant lopsided democracy of electoral competition without checks and balances is likely to misuse its opportunities in ways that make it fail to grow. This in turn closes off the path that most societies have taken to building a balanced form of democracy, namely, through economic development. The resource trap may well extend beyond the bottom billion. Many of the middle-income, resource-rich societies, notably Russia, Venezuela, and countries in the Middle East, could well be caught in it. At least for their citizens life is not as miserable as in the bottom billion, because they are stagnant at middle-income levels rather than being stagnant at the bottom. So I want to suggest not that the resource trap is unique to the bottom billion, just that it is important to them.

Why It Matters for G8 Policy

Citizens of the G8 are less likely to think "so what?" about the natural resource trap than about the conflict trap. Very obviously, failures in resource-rich countries impinge on the rest of us—Iraq is certainly an example of that. They also represent a massive waste of the money that we are paying these countries to buy their resources. As I will discuss in Chapter 7, the payments are far larger than aid, and they are far less effective in generating economic development.

Even if you do not care about your money being wasted as long as you can buy the natural resources, you need to worry about the resource curse. It is a commonplace that the rich world wants to shift its dependence on oil away from the Middle East. That is where Africa and Central Asia come in. Yet it is also a commonplace that one reason why the Middle East is in such difficulties is that it has had such large oil revenues. Shifting our source of supply simply will not work as a security measure if the resource curse shifts with it. Becoming reliant upon the bottom billion for natural resources sounds to me like *Middle East 2*. Fortunately, precisely because we are intimately involved in the resource trap as its paymasters, we have instruments ready at hand to break it; we just have not got around to using them. I am going to argue in Chapter 9 that it is not mere chance that we have not tried to fix the problem; the resource trap has two ends, and we are stuck at one of them. Each rich, resource-hungry country is locked into a prisoner's dilemma of inaction. But first I will turn to another trap.

CHAPTER 4

Landlocked with Bad Neighbors

ONE DAY, while I was director of the research department of the World Bank, a young Ghanaian came to see me. He was working in the Central African Republic as the economic advisor to the prime minister. That alone tells you something about the Central African Republic—the prime minister could not find a national to be his economic advisor. The country had produced scarcely any educated people, and years of bad governance had induced these few to flee. Even the prime minister was a returned exile. Anyway, this serious-minded young man had read my work and wanted advice on what the country could possibly do to get out of stagnation. Eventually, in 2002, I paid a visit to the country, where at the airport I was met by a crew from the national television station as if I were a celebrity. That also tells you something—that nobody visits the Central African Republic. When I settled into discussions with the government, I asked them a question that I always ask when advising a government, because it forces people to get concrete and also serves as a measure of ambition: which country did they wish to be like in twenty years' time? The group of government ministers discussed it among themselves for a while, then turned back to me with the answer: Burkina Faso. Burkina Faso! In fact, it was not a foolish answer by any means. The two countries share some important characteristics, and Burkina Faso has been doing about as well as possible given those conditions. But it remains dirt poor. That the realistic horizon of ambition for the Central African

Republic in twenty years should be to get to where Burkina Faso now is speaks of despair.

This chapter is going to be about one aspect of geography that matters for development and which condemns the Central African Republic and Burkina Faso to the slow lane. Among economists there has been a realization over the past decade that geography matters. There have been two pioneering lines of analysis in researching the importance of geography, completely different and complementary. One looks at geographic differences between places, and the scholar who pioneered this was Jeff Sachs. The other line of analysis, less intuitively, poses the question of what happens if countries all start out at the same level but some countries get in first on various opportunities. The scholars who led this work were Paul Krugman and Tony Venables. Both these sets of ideas matter a lot for understanding the problems of the bottom billion. One is going to be the subject of this chapter, and the other features in Part 3.

Sachs' work suggested that being landlocked clipped around half a percentage point off the growth rate. The standard slick response to Jeff's concerns was to point to Switzerland, Austria, or Luxembourg—or, in Africa, to Botswana, for a long time the fastest-growing country in the world. It is true that being landlocked does not necessarily condemn a country either to poverty or to slow growth, but 38 percent of the people living in bottom-billion societies are in countries that are landlocked—and, as you will see, it is overwhelmingly an African problem. Because Africa's problems are usually ascribed to its being Africa, and the rest of the world hasn't got the problem of being landlocked, the difficulties that it generates have been underplayed.

Neighbors Matter

I was lucky while directing the World Bank's research department to recruit Tony Venables to head its research division on trade, and I encouraged him to look further into the problems of being landlocked. Tony managed to find data on the cost of transporting a container from ports in the United States and Europe to capital cities around the world. Sure enough, cities that were the capitals of landlocked countries incurred much higher transport costs. However, the big surprise was that the costs varied enormously in ways that did not seem to depend upon distance. Tony eventually tracked this down. The transport costs for a landlocked country depended upon how much its coastal neighbor had spent on transport infrastructure. One way of thinking about this was that landlocked countries were hostages to their neighbors.

Why is Uganda poor when Switzerland is rich? It is indeed partly that Switzerland's access to the sea depends upon German and Italian infrastructure, whereas Uganda's access to the sea depends upon Kenyan infrastructure. Which do you imagine is better? If you are landlocked with poor transport links to the coast that are beyond your control, it is very difficult to integrate into global markets for any product that requires a lot of transport, so forget manufacturing—which to date has been the most reliable driver of rapid development.

But I wondered whether neighbors were also important in another way. Maybe landlocked countries depended upon their neighbors not just as transport corridors to overseas markets but also directly as markets. Maybe Germany and Italy were not *in the way* of Switzerland's market, they *were* Switzerland's market. Switzerland was not cut off from its market, it was surrounded by it. Well, why not Uganda? All landlocked countries are by definition surrounded by neighbors. Unfortunately, some neighbors are better as markets than others. Switzerland has Germany, Italy, France, and Austria. Uganda has Kenya, which has been stagnant for nearly three decades; Sudan, which has been embroiled in a civil war; Rwanda, which had a genocide; Somalia, which completely collapsed; the Democratic Republic of the Congo, the history of which was sufficiently catastrophic for it to change its name from Zaire; and finally Tanzania, which invaded it. You could say that at least in recent decades Switzerland has been in the better neighborhood. And as for the Central African Republic, perhaps you could take a look on a map. In principle, its lifeline should be the Oubangui River. That used to be the cost-effective way of getting out the logs that were a key export product. But, unfortunately, downstream from the Central African Republic was an area nominally part of the Democratic Republic of the Congo—civil war territory, and hence lawless. So the river could not be used and the logs were sent by road. Actually, sent by *the* road. These logs were huge. I seem to remember from somewhere that road damage increases by the cube of the axle weight. A consequence of hauling these logs by road was that it destroyed the road. I stood by the road and saw it happening.

I decided to look at this statistically. Globally, how did landlocked countries grow, and how was their growth affected by their neighbors? This time my partner was Steve O'Connell, a professor at Swarthmore College. We found that whether being landlocked mattered at all depended upon what other opportunities were open to the country. If it had a large natural resource surplus (see Chapter 3), that, rather than whether it was landlocked, became its defining feature. That is why Botswana could do so well despite being landlocked: it got the management of its huge natural resource wealth right. As we saw in the preceding chapter, if a country has a lot of natural resources, it is in all likelihood going to be uncompetitive in other exports—the theory of Dutch disease. Being coastal does not confer on a resource-rich country an export opportunity that the country would lose were it landlocked, for this opportunity has already been closed off by the resource abundance. And a landlocked resource-rich country is not at much of a disadvantage in exporting its resource wealth, since natural resources are usually so valuable that they can be exported despite the higher transport costs associated with being landlocked. Indeed, compared to the resource-scarce landlocked countries, resource-rich landlocked ones at least have the chance of making a success of the opportunity, which is what Botswana did.

So in trying to establish what characteristics are serious impediments to growth, it is evidently sensible to supplement the characteristic of being landlocked with the qualifier that this matters only for countries that are not abundant in natural resources. But this still leaves 30 percent of the bottom billion in the category.

We found that in general all countries, landlocked or not, benefited from the growth of their neighbors: growth spills over. The global average was that if a country's neighbors grew by an additional 1 percent, the country grew at an additional 0.4 percent. So nice neighborhoods, in the sense of fast growth, are pretty helpful for everyone. Globally, resource-scarce landlocked countries seem to make a special effort to piggyback on the growth of their neighbors—for the landlocked the spillover is not 0.4 percent but 0.7 percent. So countries such as Switzerland disproportionately orient their economies to serve the markets of their neighbors. If you are coastal, you serve the world; if you are landlocked, you serve your neighbors. That is fine if you are Switzerland, but it is not much use if you are Uganda, with neighbors that might be geographically more fortunate— either they are coastal or they are rich in natural resources—but for one reason or another have failed to harness their growth opportunities. To generalize that statement, resource-scarce landlocked countries must depend on their neighbors for growth (what else can they do?), but the viability of this option depends upon whether those neighbors are stuck in one or another of the growth traps.

Consider Uganda's neighbors again. Kenya and Tanzania for many years have been stuck because of poor policy, a trap we'll come to. The Democratic Republic of the Congo, Sudan, and Somalia are stuck in conflict. Rwanda is stuck in the same landlocked trap as Uganda and is not so great on conflict either. Uganda can neither access the global market, because of the high transport costs of hauling along neglected Kenyan roads, nor rely upon reorienting its economy to its neighbors, as they are stuck too.

Being both resource-scarce and landlocked, along with having neighbors who either do not have opportunities or do not take them, pretty well condemns a country to the slow lane. But are many nations stuck in this situation? Outside Africa, no. In the developing world, excluding Africa, only 1 percent of the population lives in countries that are both landlocked and resource-scarce. Another way of saying this is that other than in Africa, areas that are far from the coast and don't have resources simply don't become countries. Pretty sensible, that: such areas are so dependent upon what the neighboring areas do that it is better to be part of their polity rather than independent. But Africa is different. Around 30 percent of Africa's population lives in landlocked, resource-scarce countries. A reasonable case can be made that such places never should have become countries. However, the deed is done: these countries exist and will continue to do so.

It gets worse. Recall that globally, landlocked resource-scarce countries at least in part get around their problems by orienting their economies to maximize growth spillovers from their neighbors. Each additional 1 percent that the neighbors grow raises their growth by 0.7 percent. Again, Africa is different. Africa's landlocked countries are not oriented toward their neighbors. Both their infrastructure and their policies are oriented either to be completely inward-looking or toward the world market.

Neighbors are just in the way of the world market, not themselves the market. And this shows up in the growth spillovers. In Africa, if the neighbors grow an extra 1 percent, how much does this spill over into the growth of a landlocked country? Well, basically, it does not spill over. The world average for all countries, landlocked or not, is 0.4 percent; for the non-African landlocked it is 0.7 percent, and for the African landlocked it is 0.2 percent—virtually nothing. Of course, to date it has not mattered very much: usually in Africa the neighbors of the landlocked have barely been growing, so there has been precious little growth to spill over. But as things stand, even if the more fortunate countries started to grow, it would not help the landlocked.

I tried to do what little I could for the Central African Republic. Neither the World Bank nor the IMF had a single staffer resident in the country. I tried to get some donor interest, but a key donor said that it was not worth it because the government was facing security problems. Maybe they knew something: a few months later there was a successful coup. The former prime minister sheltered for some months in an embassy and is currently living in Paris. So now the country is in the coup trap also—it is possible to be in more than one trap at once.

So What Can a Landlocked Country Do?

Being landlocked and resource-scarce in a bad neighborhood makes development harder, but can a country develop nevertheless if its government does the right things? That was, in essence, what the prime minister of the Central African Republic wanted to know. In trying to offer an answer, we are exploring the limits of national action by the landlocked countries of the bottom billion. Landlocked, resource-scarce countries have no single obvious winning growth strategy that will take them to middle-income status, so they need to be ingenious.

Strategy 1: Increase Neighborhood Growth Spillovers

What can be done to increase growth spillovers from neighbors? Cross-border trade is primarily a matter of transport infrastructure and trade policy. However, cross-border trade depends upon the transport infrastructure on both sides of the border, so half of the problem is outside the control of the government of the landlocked country. What about trade policy? I will explore this more in Chapter 10. While the landlocked countries have a strong interest in regional integration, including the elimination of intraregional trade barriers, they also have a strong interest in reducing the external trade barriers of the region. Regional trade barriers generate an invisible transfer from the poor landlocked countries to their more industrialized and richer neighbors. Within a regional trade bloc the landlocked countries should therefore lobby for the lowest possible trade barriers. But again, that depends on the neighbors. When the East African Community revived its common external tariff in 2003, Uganda was forced to raise its trade barriers against nonmembers.

Strategy 2: Improve Neighbors' Economic Policies

An implication of spillovers is that once economies are better integrated, the economic performance of neighbors matters more. The faster neighbors grow, the faster the landlocked country will grow. Not only can the landlocked not afford to make policy mistakes, they cannot afford to have their more fortunate neighbors make mistakes. Hence, good policy choices of the more fortunately endowed neighbors are regional public goods and so tend to be undersupplied through individual national decisions. This is not a reciprocal relationship: it matters to Niger enormously that Nigeria should adopt good policies, but whether Niger adopts good policies is of little consequence for Nigeria. So Niger can plead to Nigeria, but there is not really the basis for a deal.

Strategy 3: Improve Coastal Access

Access to the sea is a vital interest for landlocked countries. But remember, the costs of access depend upon the transport infrastructure and policy decisions of coastal neighbors. Since the neighboring governments are providing a regional public good, usually they have insufficient incentive to provide as much of it as is needed.

Strategy 4: Become a Haven for the Region

Many business services are regionally traded rather than globally traded—for example, some financial services. Often these services depend upon a good policy environment. If one country in a region manages to set policies clearly superior to those of its neighbors, it will attract these services and export them around the region. The classic example of this was Lebanon, which became a financial center for the entire Middle East. As Lebanon demonstrates, a country does not need to be landlocked in order to become a regional haven. The landlocked have no absolute advantage. However, they do have a comparative advantage. Landlocked countries evidently have fewer alternative strategies than more fortunately endowed countries and so can be seen to have a stronger incentive to sustain necessary reforms. The possibility of becoming the center for regional goods that are highly policy-sensitive, such as finance, gives landlocked countries a differential incentive to adopt good policies.

Strategy 5: Don't Be Air-locked or E-locked

The technology of trade has to some extent shifted in favor of landlocked countries. Air transport is much more important than it used to be. There are significant economies of scale in air transport, and in this respect the landlocked countries are at a disadvantage because they are small markets for air services. However, low costs are possible even at modest scale; the key is deregulation. Nigeria provides a good model of how an open-skies policy can radically reduce the cost of air services and increase their frequency. Possibly these very companies might provide the foundation for a region-wide low-cost air service for landlocked Africa. More generally, the landlocked need cost-cutting companies like Ryanair, easyJet, and Southwest Airlines. What they have had is staggeringly expensive and badly run state airlines, the most celebrated being that of Zaire, whose planes were periodically commandeered for the First Lady's shopping trips.

E-services now have the potential to deliver rapid economic growth. This is the story of recent economic development in India. Because India is a coastal economy, it has many options for global integration. The landlocked do not have such a range of options. E-services are attractive because distance is irrelevant. The twin pillars of being competitive in e-services are having good telecommunications infrastructure and having workers with postprimary education. Good telecommunications depends upon getting regulatory and competition policies right. It is a relatively simple matter to tell when they are wrong: prices are too high relative to global benchmarks and coverage is inadequate.

Strategy 6: Encourage Remittances

Because landlocked economies have fewer options for growth, they are likely to experience substantial emigration. This of course depends upon the willingness of other governments to let in immigrants from the bottom billion, and in any case it leaches out the society's talent. However, emigration can be turned to some advantage through enabling migrants to make large remittances. Maximizing remittances depends upon several steps. One is to educate people so that they are employable in higher-income economies rather than simply as unskilled workers in neighboring countries that are almost as poor. Another is to facilitate the finding of jobs in such economies. A model for such practices is the Philippines, where training is targeted to the needs of high-income economies and the government provides information and embassy services to make hiring of its citizens easy. Another is to encourage emigrant workers to remit part of their incomes. This depends upon banking systems and exchange rates. An overvalued exchange rate taxes remittances and therefore discourages them. A longer-term strategy is to encourage the diaspora to invest in the country, for example, building homes for family and retirement, and linking the second-generation emigrants more closely to the country.

Strategy 7: Create a Transparent and Investor-Friendly Environment for Resource Prospecting

The area of landlocked low-income countries currently classified as resource-scarce is enormous. It seems likely that there are valuable resources in the ground that have not yet been discovered. The main impediment to prospecting is likely to be the risks perceived by resource extraction companies. Some of these are political, but the more important one is probably the risk to the reputation of the company should the host country's governance of the resource revenues become manifestly problematic. Not all companies are concerned about the risk to their reputation because not all companies have good reputations to protect. However, this gives rise to what is known technically as an "adverse selection problem": the companies attracted to the risky environments are those that are not concerned about poor governance and so have no interest in helping to avoid the problems of the resource trap. This adverse selection is now extending to the governments behind many resource extraction companies. In 2006 the vice president of China toured Africa with the revealing refrain "We won't ask questions."

Strategy 8: Rural Development

Because landlocked countries do not have the option of rapid industrialization, the bulk of their populations will continue to be rural for a long time. In turn, this implies that policies for rural development should receive higher priority than in other economies. Whereas the policies needed for industrial exports are pretty standard around the world, policies for rural development must be adapted to local circumstances and so require a much larger investment in local knowledge. A further constraint upon rural development is the subsidies that are paid to farmers in Europe, Japan, and the United States.

Strategy 9: Try to Attract Aid

Even with a government's best efforts at these strategies, the country is likely to stay poor for a long time. So it should try to be as attractive as possible to donors. I take this up in Chapter 9.

Why It Matters for G8 Policy

As you will have noticed, most of these strategies are not under the full control of a country's government. It is dependent upon its neighbors, or upon international actors such as donors. Still, a good government can most surely make a difference in a landlocked resource-scarce country, even with bad neighbors. For example, governments in Uganda and Burkina Faso have sustained decent growth rates for over a decade, though some of this was recovery from the damage of terrible predecessors. But I can find no example of a landlocked, resource-scarce country with bad neighbors that has made it to middle-income status. They will be stuck in poverty unless we help them far more than we have to date. How to help them is one of the questions I address in Part 4.

CHAPTER 5

Bad Governance in a Small Country

GOVERNANCE AND ECONOMIC POLICIES help to shape economic performance, but there is an asymmetry in the consequences of getting them right and getting them wrong. Excellent governance and economic policies can help the growth process, but there is a ceiling to feasible growth rates at around 10 percent: economies just cannot grow much faster than this no matter what governments do. By contrast, terrible governance and policies can destroy an economy with alarming speed. For example, President Robert Mugabe must take responsibility for the economic collapse in Zimbabwe since 1998, culminating in inflation of over 1,000 percent a year. That decline is visible from the moment you set foot in the country and walk through its deserted international airport. Because of this asymmetry, the implementation of restraints is likely to be even more important than the promotion of government effectiveness.

I think that the advocates of good governance and the advocates of good policies—rather different groups of people—have both somewhat oversold their wares. Good governance and policy help a country to realize its opportunities, but they cannot generate opportunities where none exist, and they cannot defy gravity. Even the best governance and policies are not going to turn Malawi into a rich country—it just does not have the opportunities. Until recently, Nigeria's best phase of economic policy (which was less than wonderful) was the reform phase of the late 1980s, but the benefits of these reforms were completely swamped by the coincident crash in the world price of oil.

Although really bad governance and policies can ruin the most promising prospects, even here qualifiers are necessary. An obvious one is that in the short term, if the external shocks such as export prices are sufficiently favorable, a society can get away with them. To an extent Nigeria did this during the first oil boom of 1974–86, and President Hugo Chávez is repeating this experience in Venezuela today. A less obvious but more important qualifier is that governance and policies are multidimensional, and not all dimensions matter in all circumstances. In the 2005 Transparency International ratings of corruption, two societies tied for global bottom place: Bangladesh and Chad. There is no doubting that both of these countries suffer from bad governance. The amazing thing is that being the most corrupt country on earth has not prevented Bangladesh from adopting fairly reasonable economic policies and from growing. One interpretation might be that it is economic policies such as exchange rates and tariffs that matter, rather than whether public officials are honest and competent, but I do not believe this is the right interpretation; rather, I think that what matters is determined by differences in opportunities. Although Bangladesh would surely have done much better had it been less corrupt, it is a classic case of a resource-scarce, coastal, low-income country. At least since the 1980s the development path for such countries has been pretty clear: export labor-intensive manufactures and services. Such a development strategy need not be very demanding of government. Even the "minimal state" model of government that was briefly promoted by the World Bank in the 1980s, in which the functions of government are drastically curtailed, is probably sufficient for success. The government merely has to avoid doing harm rather than actively do much good. Exporters simply need an environment of moderate taxation, macroeconomic stability, and a few transport facilities. Somehow, partly by means of export processing zones, which provide islands of better governance, the government of Bangladesh has managed to keep its bad governance from choking off export activity. Chad, by contrast, is a landlocked country with aid and oil. It has no scope for exporting, and to make use of aid and oil the government must be able to spend money effectively. For this strategy to work the government must be more ambitious than a do-no-harm approach—it must actually be capable of doing some good. The minimal state is not a viable model in the context of oil and aid; the government must transform its money into public services. Does corruption impede development given these opportunities? Of course it does. In 2004 a survey tracked money released by the Ministry of Finance in Chad intended for rural health clinics. The survey had the extremely modest purpose of finding out how much of the money actually reached the clinics—not whether the clinics spent it well, or whether the staff of the clinics knew what they were doing, just where the money went. Amazingly, less that 1 percent of it reached the clinics—99 percent failed to reach its destination. Bad governance matters in Chad more than in Bangladesh, because Chad's only option is for government to provide services, and corruption has closed off this option.

So governance and policies matter, conditional upon opportunities. But how do we tell whether governance and policies are adequate? Assessment of these is subjective and can be controversial. Does France have worse governance than the United States? Are Sweden's economic policies better than those of Britain? Fortunately, controversy greatly diminishes by the time we reach the countries of the bottom billion: nobody seriously doubts that Angola has worse governance than India, or that Chad has worse economic policies than China.

Bad policies and governance need not be a trap: societies can learn from failure, and many do. The most dramatic error correction of modern times has occurred in China. In the 1960s Mao Zedong hurled China into ruin, to an adoring chorus from the Western media. But in response to failure the Chinese political elite swung policy 180 degrees and generated the biggest economic success in history (Mao made his own invaluable contribution by dropping dead). In part spurred by China, India followed. Why have China and India, and indeed many other countries, changed policies while others have not? Why is bad governance so persistent in some environments?

One evident reason is that not everybody loses from it. The leaders of many of the poorest countries in the world are themselves among the global superrich. They like things the way they are, and so it pays to keep their citizens uneducated and ill-informed. Unfortunately, many of the politicians and senior public officials in the countries of the bottom billion are villains. But persistence is not just due to self-interest. Among the politicians and officials many are people of integrity, and sometimes against the odds they gain the upper hand. These are the moments of reform. But economic reform is not just a matter of political will. It is also a technical matter, and in the bottom billion there is a chronic shortage of people with the requisite knowledge. Few citizens get the training needed, and those who do get it leave. All too often, brave reformers get overwhelmed by the forces pitted against them before they can see a strategy through to completion. And finally, there is not much popular enthusiasm for economic reform because it has got a bad name. In the 1980s the international financial institutions tried to coerce governments into reform through "conditionality"—a government could get extra aid only if it agreed to change some of its economic policies. Nobody likes being coerced, least of all newly powerful local elites that are hypersensitive about sovereignty and see their gravy trains threatened. Conditionality turned out to be a paper tiger: governments discovered they only needed to *promise* to reform, not actually do it. Meanwhile, the Western left, locked in its domestic struggle with U.S. president Ronald Reagan and British prime minister Margaret Thatcher, conflated the limited reforms being urged on the governments of the bottom billion with the neoliberal savaging of the state they were fighting at home. As a result, reforms that should have been popular with all except corrupt elites became toxic in the media both within and outside Africa. The essential struggle between villains and heroes within the bottom billion became twisted into one between Africa and the IMF.

What determines the pace of reform starting from a situation in which governance and policy is undeniably bad? In effect, what determines whether the villains or the heroes win the power struggle? To conduct a statistical analysis, Lisa Chauvet, a young French researcher, and I needed to reduce amorphous entities such as governance and policies to numerical scores. We used an index called the Country Policy and Institutional Assessment, produced by the World Bank. At the time we did the work the index was not publicly available; however, the World Bank wanted to know what might promote turnarounds and so released the data to us for the purposes of the study. (The Bank's board subsequently decided to make it publicly available as of 2006.) The index has several important advantages: it provides data for a long period and is intended to be comparable across countries. It also has the disadvantage of being subjective, but since objective quantitative measures are available only as occasional snapshots, there is no realistic alternative. Possibly its main drawback for our purposes is that it can be gamed by the staff who are making the judgment: a higher rating attracts a larger lending program, and this can be advantageous to the staff concerned. Both in principle and in practice such manipulation is policed, but it is unlikely to have been eliminated.

The scoring system rates twenty aspects of governance and policy on a six-point scale. We imposed a low cutoff to define the really bad. I doubt if there is much professional disagreement that the countries that fall below this cutoff indeed have really poor governance and policies. There will undoubtedly be disagreement in the sense that some countries that do not fall below the cutoff nevertheless have severe problems. For example, despite being highly corrupt, on this measure Bangladesh overall has economic policies that are comfortably above the cutoff. It was not always that way: Bangladesh is one of the countries that very slowly inched its way from a truly dreadful configuration of policies and governance to one that, though still poor, is manifestly not debilitating for growth.

For want of a better term I will call those low-income countries that are below the cutoff for governance and economic policies "failing states." This is the sort of popular and emotive term that I do not usually like to use, but in this case I think it has some rationale. Such states are failing in two senses. Most directly, they are failing their citizens. Populations in most of the low-income world live in countries that are growing rapidly, whereas these countries are stagnating. Yet more troubling is that low-income countries that fail to grow are living dangerously, as we saw in Chapter 2.

Getting the definition right is nevertheless tricky. Not all low-income states that fall below our cutoff have been failing states. For a number of countries, the rating crashed and then rapidly rebounded as policies changed relatively rapidly. Such temporary crashes are not of interest to us. It is surely much easier to restore a country to reasonable policies if it has only just abandoned them than if it has been stuck with bad policies for a long time. Indeed, the temporary crashes we observe in the data may sometimes be spurious assessments that are subsequently reversed. We therefore only count the country as a failing state if the rating has stayed low for a continuous period of four years.

These criteria give us lists of states that can be classified as failing, year by year. To show you what they mean in practice, recent failing states include Angola, the Central African Republic, Haiti, Liberia, Sudan, the Solomon Islands, Somalia, and Zimbabwe. It would surely be difficult to argue with any of these assessments. The Democratic Republic of the Congo hovers around the borderline. If this is the borderline, you know that the cutoff is low. More than three-quarters of the population of the bottom billion live in countries that have at some time been failing states by this definition.

Do Failing States Turn Around of Their Own Accord?

Launching a turnaround takes courage. I cannot measure that and so it is not going to be included in my analysis, but behind the moments of change there are always a few people within these societies who have decided to try to make a difference. Successful turnarounds are not common, but this does not usually imply a want of courage. I remember meeting the brave man who had told President Hastings Banda, the dictator of Malawi, that his policies were failing. This man (who also was called Banda, though he was not related to the president) had explained to the president that Press Holdings, the state within a state that Banda ran as his personal property, was heading for ruin. This evidence was a necessary first step in persuading the president to change policies. Given Banda's record, it was risky: the president was far from being a fool, but he hated opposition. The country was headed straight for crisis unless he was faced with the facts, but facing him with the facts might backfire. It was a situation that required courage, and courage was forthcoming. President Banda did not shoot Banda the messenger; he jailed him. Courage earned this man twelve years in a prison cell. Turnarounds are rare because reformers are often suppressed and sometimes pay a high price for their efforts. In the long march through the statistical evidence that follows, try not to lose sight of what attempts at reform actually involve.

If we were to study turnarounds statistically, we had to define them. Of course the simplest criterion would be the converse of the conditions for state failure, but this would rapidly lead to absurdities. If the rating rises from a long stay just below the cutoff to just above it, we do not want to regard this as a turnaround. Given the subjective nature of the rating, such small improvements might be entirely spurious, and even if they are genuine they hardly constitute a significant event. We therefore confined ourselves to turnarounds that were so large as to be unmistakable. We allowed a turnaround to be achieved over any time period. Bangladesh is an example of a very gradual turnaround: there is no dramatic "event" worthy of particular notice, but over a quarter century policies and some institutions improved from abysmal to adequate (though governance did not, as you will recall).

However, a large improvement is not enough; it must be sustained. We decided to define "sustained" as being at least five years. Had we chosen a very long period of sustained improvement, we would have excluded situations such as in Indonesia. The improvement in Indonesia began in 1967 and was broadly sustained until the collapse associated with the Asian financial crisis of 1998. It seemed to us unreasonable to attribute that collapse to failures in the original reforms.

Having established what we meant by a turnaround in a failing state, we were at last ready to investigate what generated them. We first investigated the preconditions for a turnaround and then tried to find out what determined whether a turnaround, once it had started, progressed to a decisive escape from being a failing state.

The Preconditions for Turnarounds

To establish the preconditions for a turnaround is technically a little like establishing the preconditions for a civil war. We estimated the probability of a turnaround, year by year, among all the potential turnaround countries and searched among a wide range of potential characteristics for those that mattered. Somewhat to our surprise, we could find only three characteristics that were reliably significant in determining whether a turnaround occurred. Starting from being a failing state, a country was more likely to achieve a sustained turnaround the larger its population, the greater the proportion of its population that had secondary education, and—perhaps more surprisingly—if it had recently emerged from civil war. Among the many characteristics that did not seem to matter one way or the other were democracy and political rights. Let's go through that list again, more slowly. Democracy doesn't seem to help policy turnaround. That is extremely disappointing, both for advocates of democracy and because democracy is more common now in the countries of the bottom billion than it used to be. Having a large population and having a high proportion of people with secondary education both help. They may well be pointing to the same thing: countries need a critical mass of educated people in order to work out and implement a reform strategy. The impetus for change must come from within the society—the heroes. Their chances of success depend on the capacities of those around them. For example, China under Mao Zedong and Tanzania under Julius Nyerere both failed, and indeed failed through somewhat similar strategies. The Chinese elite was able to rethink and adopt a radically different strategy. There were also Tanzanians of ability and courage who pressed for change and who eventually triumphed, but in the 1980s there were not enough of them, and it did not help that they were opposed by Western Marxists who flattered the government into complacency. (I remember one of the reformers saying, "If they think it's so wonderful, why don't they come and live here?")

Finally, there is the odd-looking result that reform is more likely after civil war. Actually, it is not so odd. Typically, although postconflict countries start off with dreadful governance and policies, that first decade sees substantial improvement. The politics are unusually fluid because the old interests have been shaken up, so it is relatively easy to get change. I am going to return to that in Part 4, when we look at interventions.

And now for the bad news. Overall, we find that the probability of a sustained turnaround starting in any year is very low: a mere 1.6 percent. Countries are therefore likely to stay as failing states for a long time. Indeed, from this annual probability we can calculate something called the mathematical expectation, which is the average length of time it takes to get out of being a failing state. It comes out as fifty-nine years.

Incipient Turnarounds

We also looked at the early stages of a reform to see what determined whether momentum was sustained. Improvements might continue right through to a decisive escape from the trap, or they might collapse, with the country reverting to its initial state. Or the country might just stall, staying in limbo for year after year. We first faced the issue of how to define an incipient turnaround. We ended up investigating two different situations, one in which a turnaround had already gotten started but not gone very far, and another in which a new president had just come into office. Although the question of what sustains incipient turnarounds sounds virtually the same as what gets them going, technically the two require a completely different approach. This question is about what is happening as time rolls by, whereas the preconditions can be reduced to a simple world of before and after.

So what did we find? Here I will differentiate between external interventions that work, which I will discuss in Part 4, and characteristics that need to exist for those interventions to work. There were six of these characteristics that actually seemed to matter. An incipient reform was more likely to progress to a sustained turnaround if the country had higher income, a larger population, and a greater proportion of the population with education. It was less likely to progress if the leader had been in office a long time, if the country experienced a favorable shift in the terms of trade, and if it had recently emerged from civil war.

Compared with the preconditions for a turnaround, there are some striking similarities and one striking difference. The similarities: countries with large and educated populations are doubly blessed, for turnarounds are both more likely to get launched and more likely to succeed once launched. The sharp difference is the postconflict experience. Postconflict countries are more likely to achieve a sustained turnaround, but any particular incipient reform is less likely to progress. How can these two seemingly contradictory results be reconciled? I think that what they are telling us is that postconflict situations are highly fluid. Some sort of reform is much more likely to be initiated in postconflict states than in other failing states, but many of these incipient reforms will fail because it is harder to sustain any continuous course of change. This suggests that there is an important difference between postconflict situations and other failing states. Recall the depressing statistic that the expected time before a failing state achieves decisive change is fifty-nine years. The normal condition for a failing state is to be stuck, as bad policies and governance are highly persistent. Postconflict situations are the major exception: they are failing states, but change is relatively easy. This suggests that our policy interventions to help failing states need to differentiate between types of situations, treating postconflict situations as major opportunities. I will have more to say on that in Part 4.

The Costs of Neglect: Why It Matters for G8 Policy

The typical failing state is going to go on failing for a long time. Does it matter? The whole topic of failing states is fashionable because people have an uneasy sense that it probably does matter. After 9/11 the U.S. aid budget was increased by 50 percent, and the main impetus for it was the perceived need to fix failing states. In Part 4 you will see how, ironically, this is what aid is *not* going to do. But can we get beyond that inchoate sense that failing states are a problem? Can we actually quantify the costs of a failing state?

Remember, I have defined a failing state in terms of its bad policies and governance. The core of the cost is what results from these policy and governance failings for the economy of the country itself and for its neighbors. Lisa Chauvet and I decided to estimate a lower bound to these costs, leaving out a lot of the consequences of state failure that are legitimate objects of concern. For example, we omitted the security costs implied by an increased risk of civil war, and the human costs implied by avoidably high infant mortality. To give some sense of how much we left out, remember that in Chapter 2, I put a figure of around $64 billion for the typical cost to a region of a civil war. To avoid double counting of the cost of the traps, here I'm going to stick to the cost of a failing state that remains at peace.

To estimate the economic cost of being a failing state required yet another battery of techniques. This took time, and the pressure was building, since our work was being financed by a consortium of donors. Like many people in the policy world, they commissioned the work at the point where they realized they needed answers, and so they wanted the answers quickly. The policy world is deeply suspicious of the world of research, often for good reason—with this sort of work there is no "progress" in the sense of usable results until pretty late in the day. And it is risky, because sometimes the data turn out not to be adequate to answer the question, and so the whole effort is wasted. In this case, fortunately, we got results that were surprisingly robust.

The costs of a failing state build up year by year. The growth rate of the failing state is very sharply reduced—indeed, it is likely to be in absolute decline. And the growth of neighbors is also sharply reduced. Since failing states take such a long time to turn around, these costs continue way into the future. Economists routinely convert flows of future costs into a single number, which they term a "discounted present value." We estimated that the cost of a single failing state over its entire history of failure, to itself and its neighbors, is around $100 billion. This is our lower-bound estimate of what a sustained turnaround is worth. It is a mesmerizingly large number, but then, the phenomenon we are considering is indeed dramatic: a world without failing states would be a transformed world. Is the figure ridiculous? I think that there is a good case for saying that it is too low, for it considers only the costs to the country itself and its neighbors.

To infer how rich countries value turnarounds, look at Iraq. The U.S.-led military intervention in Iraq provides us with a rare opportunity to calculate what a key international actor regarded as the benefits to itself of one sustained turnaround. The purpose of the intervention was clearly stated as being regime change. The regime in Iraq was a classic example of a failing but politically secure state, so the costs of state failure could reasonably be seen as likely to be highly persistent. The military intervention in Iraq has already cost around $350 billion, but let's look at what the initial estimates were. Before the war began, costs of at least $100 billion could readily be forecast. The decision to intervene in Iraq implies expected benefits of intervention in excess of these anticipated costs. Further, the expected benefits of intervention to promote a turnaround depend upon the value of the turnaround, but this value has to be reduced by the probability that the desired turnaround will fail. If the turnaround has only a 50 percent chance of success, then the expected value of the intervention is only half the benefits of the turnaround. So we know that for the intervention in Iraq the expected value must have exceeded the expected costs of intervention, and so been valued at more than $100 billion. If the George W. Bush administration had applied any discount for the prospects that a new Iraqi regime would revert to state failure, the valuation placed on a successful turnaround would necessarily be higher than the costs of military intervention. Clearly, the U.S.-led intervention in Iraq is unusual in many respects; as the costs escalate it looks increasingly like a mistake. But my point is not to try to make a cost-benefit analysis of intervention in Iraq, let alone consider its wider political context. Rather, it is to suggest that the value of a successful state turnaround to the international community is very large.

So if you support the Iraq war, you have to agree that the benefits of turning around a failing state are enormous. But the converse does not follow. If you are opposed to the war in Iraq, it most probably does not mean that you do not value turnarounds in failing states. It is more likely to mean that you are concerned about the actual costs of what you regard as a doubtful military intervention. Pose the following question: how much would it have been worth to have Iraqis themselves throw out Saddam Hussein and install a stable replacement?

In Part 4 I am going to look at nonmilitary interventions to turn around failing states—essentially, interventions that support local efforts at change. Typically, intelligent external support is going to raise the chances of a turnaround, but any particular reform effort is nevertheless likely to fail. One way of thinking of this is that we can shorten the time that a failing state is stuck. These interventions are going to cost money. Whether they are worth the money depends upon how much they increase the chances of sustaining a turnaround, and how much a successful turnaround is worth. If turning around a failing state is anything like as valuable as I think it is—worth $100 billion to the region, and perhaps more than that to the rest of the world—even small improvements in probabilities are well worthwhile. As I will discuss later, Lisa and I think that we have found a nonmilitary intervention that becomes worth doing even if a successful turnaround is valued at only $7 billion. In other words, we think we have found a bargain, though the world is not yet doing it, at least not on any large scale.

Part 3

An Interlude: Globalization to the Rescue?

On Missing the Boat: The Marginalization of the Bottom Billion in the World Economy

ALL THE PEOPLE LIVING in the countries of the bottom billion have been in one or another of the traps that I have described in the preceding four chapters. Seventy-three percent of them have been through civil war, 29 percent of them are in countries dominated by the politics of natural resource revenues, 30 percent are landlocked, resource-scarce, and in a bad neighborhood, and 76 percent have been through a prolonged period of bad governance and poor economic policies. Adding up these percentages, you will realize that some countries have been in more than one trap, either simultaneously or sequentially.

But when I speak of traps, I am speaking figuratively. These traps are probabilistic; unlike black holes, it is not impossible to escape from them, just difficult. Take as an example the trap of bad governance and poor policies, and remember that the mathematical expectation of being stuck with bad policies is nearly sixty years. That expectation is built up from the very small chance, less than 2 percent, of escaping from the trap in any single year. But of course that small change implies that periodically countries do escape. This is true of all the traps: a peace holds (as is currently the case in Angola), natural resources get depleted (as is looming in Cameroon, which has nearly exhausted its oil reserves), reformers succeed in transforming governance and policies (as is now under way in Nigeria). And such transformations have implications for the landlocked: as Nigeria turns itself around, Niger, though still landlocked, is now in a better neighborhood. The focus of this chapter is to ask what happens next.

You might think that if a country escapes from a trap, it can then start to catch up—it will begin to grow, and grow pretty fast. The professional term for catch-up is "convergence." The best-studied example of convergence is the European Union. The countries that were initially the poorest members, such as Portugal, Ireland, and Spain, have grown the fastest, whereas the country that was initially richest, Germany, has grown slowly, and so the states that make up the European Union have converged. That is partly why relatively poor countries such as Poland and the other countries of Eastern Europe have been keen to join, whereas the countries that are richer than the European Union, Norway and Switzerland, have decided not to do so. Convergence is also working on a global scale: the lower-income countries are, on the whole, growing faster than the developed countries. People in the developed world are starting to get worried that China is converging on us so fast. The fact that the countries of the bottom billion have bucked this trend to convergence is the puzzle with which I started. And so far my explanation has been that they have been stuck in one or another of the four traps.

Will the countries that emerge from the traps follow the path blazed by the successful majority of developing countries? Will they join the rush to convergence? Globalization arouses passions: it is considered either wonderful or terrible. I think the sad reality is that although globalization has powered the majority of developing countries toward prosperity, it is now making things harder for these latecomers. The purpose of this chapter is to explain why the countries of the bottom billion have missed the boat.

What is globalization? Its effects on the economies of developing countries come from three distinct processes. One is trade in goods, the second is flows of capital, and the third is the migration of people. The three aspects of globalization are so distinct that even the idea that economies have become more globalized depends upon which dimensions you take. In terms of both capital movements and migration, the developing countries were more globalized a century ago than they are now. It is only trade in goods that has grown to unprecedented levels. And even that has not been a continuous process. Between 1914 and 1945 world trade collapsed because of wars and protectionism. It is often said that globalization is inevitable, but those interwar years cast doubt on this assertion: for those who hate globalization, the retreat of trade, capital flows, and migration during the period 1914–45 should be interesting because they are a kind of a natural experiment. Unfortunately, they were a ghastly experiment: the reversal of globalization, though feasible, looks massively undesirable based on the one occasion when we did it.

But the consequences of globalization for the bottom billion are different. Let's take the three aspects of globalization in turn, and see how they affect the bottom billion.

Trade and the Bottom Billion

International trade has taken place for several thousand years. However, the most dramatic transformation of the size and composition of trade has been during the past twenty-five years. For the first time in history, developing countries have broken into global markets for goods and services other than just primary commodities. Until around 1980 developing countries' role was to export raw materials. Now, 80 percent of developing countries' exports are manufactures, and service exports are also mushrooming. The production of primary commodities is basically land-using, and exporting them is most likely to benefit the people who own the land. Sometimes the land is owned by peasant farmers, but often the key beneficiaries are mining companies and big landowners. So trade based on primary commodity exporting is likely to generate quite a lot of income inequality. And its scope is inherently limited by the size of the market: as exports grow, prices turn against exporters. By contrast, manufactures and services offer much better prospects of equitable and rapid development. They use labor rather than land. The opportunity to export raises the demand for labor. Since the defining characteristic of developing countries is that they have a lot of unproductive labor, these exports are likely to spread the benefits of development more widely. And because the world market in manufactures and services is huge and was initially dominated by the rich countries, the scope for expansion by developing countries is massive.

However, before getting starry-eyed about this transformation in developing countries' trade, let us ask why it took so long. In the 1960s and

1970s the rich world dominated global manufacturing despite having wages that were around forty times as high as those in the developing world. Why did this massive wage gap not make developing countries competitive? Part of the answer is that the rich world imposed trade restrictions on the poor world. Another part of the answer is that the poor world shot itself in the foot with its own trade restrictions, which made exporting into a competitive world market unprofitable. But trade restrictions are only part of the explanation for the persistence of the wage gap for so long. The more important explanation is that the rich world could get away with a big wage gap because there are spatial economies of scale in manufacturing. That is, if other firms are producing manufactures in the same location, that tends to lower the costs for your firm. For example, with lots of firms doing the same thing, there will be a pool of workers with the skills that your firm needs. And there will be plenty of firms producing the services and inputs that you need to function efficiently. Try moving to someplace where there are no other firms, and these costs are going to be much higher even if raw labor is much cheaper.

The professional term for this is "economies of agglomeration." It was the key building block for the big insight of Paul Krugman and Tony Venables. They asked what would happen if the wage gap widened until it became big enough to offset this advantage from scale economies. Imagine yourself as the first firm successfully to jump the wage gap—that is, you relocate from the high-wage world to the low-wage world. At first you do not make a fortune. You just about break even—if by moving it was possible to instantly make a fortune, someone else would already have done so. You are the first to move and not go bankrupt, and you just get by. It is lonely being the first firm; there are no other firms around to generate those agglomeration economies, but you just hang on. And now here comes the important step. How do things look to a second firm that is thinking of relocating? Well, for the second firm it all looks a bit better than it did for the first firm because there is already another firm there. So the second firm relocates. And that also helps the first firm. They both start to do better than just getting by. And the third firm? Better still. What happens is an explosive shift of manufacturing to the new location. Does this sound familiar—like the shift of manufacturing from the United States and Europe to Asia? The change has been explosive because once activity started to relocate, agglomerations grew in low-wage Asia. In the process, wages are being driven up in Asia, but the gap was initially enormous and there is a huge amount of cheap labor in Asia, and so this process of convergence is going to run for many more years. I have described it as firms relocating. Sometimes this is precisely what happens—outsourcing, or "delocalization." But it need not be, and you do not stop it by banning firms from moving. It could equally well be that new firms set up in the low-wage locations and outcompete the existing firms in the high-wage locations. Firms do not have to move in order for industrial activity to shift location, since births of firms in one place and deaths of firms in another come to the same thing.

In effect, in order to break into global markets for manufactures it is necessary to get over a threshold of cost-competitiveness. If only a country can get over the threshold, it enjoys virtually infinite possibilities of expansion: if the first firm is profitable, so are its imitators. This expansion creates jobs, especially for youth. Admittedly, the jobs are far from wonderful, but they are an improvement on the drudgery and boredom of a small farm, or of hanging around on a street corner trying to sell cigarettes. As jobs become plentiful they provide a degree of economic security not just for the people who get them but for the families behind the workers. And gradually, as jobs expand, the labor market tightens and wages start to rise. This started to happen in Madagascar in the late 1990s. The government established an export processing zone and created policies good enough that firms were sufficiently cost-competitive to take advantage of an American trade arrangement called the Africa Growth and Opportunity Act. Almost overnight the zone grew from very few jobs to 300,000 jobs. That is a lot of jobs in a country with only 15 million people. The jobs would probably have kept on growing, but politics got in the way. When the president, Admiral Didier Ratsiraka, lost the election he refused to step down, and he got his cronies to blockade the port, a city his supporters controlled. For eight months the worthy admiral attempted to get his job back through economic strangulation of the wayward electorate. Unsurprisingly, by then the export processing zone had been decimated. By the time it restarted there were only 40,000 jobs and firms were wary of returning. I remember a manager of an American garment company telling me in disbelief that the former president had chosen to wreck his own country. He said, "If it's like that, then count us out. We'll stick to Asia."

Madagascar is a country of the bottom billion that in the 1990s almost broke into world markets. How about the bottom billion more generally? In this initial shift out of Europe and America the bottom billion are those low-income countries that for one reason or another did not get chosen by firms as a good place to relocate. How has this affected their chances of convergence? It suggests to me that there was a moment—roughly the decade of the 1980s—when the wage gap was sufficiently wide that any low-wage developing country could break into global markets as long as it was not stuck in one of the traps. During the 1990s this opportunity receded because Asia was building agglomerations of manufactures and services. These agglomerations became fabulously competitive: low wages combined with scale economies. Neither the rich countries nor the bottom billion could compete. The rich countries did not have low wages, and the bottom billion, which surely had low wages, did not have the agglomerations. They had missed the boat.

I decided to try to test this out empirically. This time my co-researcher was Steve O'Connell, who had already worked with me on the problems of the landlocked. Our question was whether the bottom billion had shot themselves in the foot during the 1980s, closing off their opportunities for export diversification.

So far, we have only looked at Africa itself, not "Africa+." That is because Steve and I did this work in the context of an African research network: the African Economic Research Consortium. I expect that what is true of Africa will turn out to be true of the rest of the bottom billion. Generally, I find that there is no "Africa effect": Africa often looks distinctive because it is dominated by the characteristics of the bottom billion. However, it is an empirical matter, and I might turn out to be wrong.

First of all, recall that Africa is disproportionately either landlocked or resource-rich. For different reasons, these two categories are very likely to be out of the game as far as export diversification is concerned. In the rest of the developing world the two groups combined account for only 12 percent of the population. In Africa they account for two-thirds of the population. Therefore, even if all of Africa's coastal, resource-scarce societies had been ready to break into global markets in the 1980s, two-thirds of the population of the region would have been left out. But were the coastal, resource-scarce economies ready to diversify into global markets? This was the group for which the issue of shooting themselves in the foot arose. Steve and I applied a classification that a group of us had developed to describe debilitating configurations of governance and policy: we considered them failing states, as defined in Chapter 5. During the 1980s only 4 percent of the population of Africa's coastal, resource-scarce countries were in countries that were free of these debilitating configurations. In fact, it comes down to Mauritius and not much else. So if you were a firm looking to relocate to a cheap labor country in the 1980s you might have chosen Mauritius, and indeed many firms did, but you were unlikely to have chosen anywhere else in Africa.

But would firms have chosen Africa even if governance and policies had been better? This sort of counterfactual question is difficult to tackle. Steve and I approached it by investigating whether those of Africa's coastal, resource-scarce countries that had subsequently escaped from being failing states had been able to diversify their exports. We found that each year of being free of the gross failures of governance and policy added significantly to the success of export diversification. The countries that stopped shooting themselves in the foot were able to break into new export markets. This is encouraging. It suggests that although Africa's coastal countries did indeed shoot themselves in the foot during the 1980s, they might still be able to break into global markets. It seems likely, however, that the process of breaking in is now harder than before Asia managed to establish itself on the scene.

If there really has been a process of missing the boat, it is pretty depressing. For one thing, it implies that the incentive for governments in the bottom-billion countries to reform, make peace, or do whatever else is needed to break free of the traps is greatly reduced. Courageous people face down the powerful interests lined up against them and implement reform only to find that little happens. The reactions to reforms that do not deliver economic success can be ugly. All the old vested interests have their knives out to kill off reform attempts. Another type of reaction is the quack remedy: people are liable to become victims of populism. The most depressing reaction is for people to see the society as intrinsically flawed. Their prolonged period of economic failure in Africa and the other countries of the bottom billion has deeply eroded the self-confidence of their societies. The expectation of continued failure reinforces the pressures for the brightest people to leave.

In Part 4, I will be arguing that this bleak prospect is not inevitable. There is something that can be done about it: we need to get serious about supporting the heroes in the struggle that is already being waged within the societies of the bottom billion. But for the moment stick with the world as it is, and let's see how it is likely to play out. When will the boat come around again? That is, when will the bottom billion actually be able to break into global markets? The automatic processes of the global economy will eventually bring the boat back around. But the bottom billion will have to wait a long time until development in Asia creates a wage gap with the bottom billion similar to the massive gap that prevailed between Asia and the rich world around 1980. This does not mean that development in the bottom billion is impossible, but it does make it much harder. The same automatic processes that drove Asian development will impede the development of the bottom billion.

So the growth of agglomerations in Asia has made the export diversification route more difficult for the bottom billion. Another effect of this growth is that Asians are increasingly desperate to secure supplies of natural resources. The Chinese are all over the countries of the bottom billion, securing natural resource deals. Superficially this is good news: it is certainly raising prices, most obviously of oil, which some countries of the bottom billion export. But you saw in Chapter 5, on the trap of poor policy, that high prices for resource exports are likely to chill the impetus for reform. In Chapter 2, on the conflict trap, you saw that the spread of high natural resource prices increased the risk of conflict. And you saw in Chapter 3, on the natural resource trap, that natural resources are not the royal road to growth unless governance is unusually good. In the bottom billion it is already unusually bad, and the Chinese are making it worse, for they are none too sensitive when it comes to matters of governance. When Zimbabwe's Robert Mugabe was looking for money to bail himself out of the ruinous consequences of his political choices, he came up with the "look east" strategy. East did not mean Russia, it meant China. And China has welcomed his overtures with open arms. The same goes for Angola.

After the defeat of Jonas Savimbi's UNITA, the developed countries finally decided to put the squeeze on the government of Angola, trying to clean up grotesque misuse of the oil money. China came in with over $4 billion in loans, and the Angolan government was off the hook. So the bottom billion are locked into natural resource exports twice over: by the threshold effects of Asian export agglomerations and by Asia's desperate need for natural resources.

The growth of global trade has been wonderful for Asia. But don't count on trade to help the bottom billion. Based on present trends, it seems more likely to lock yet more of the bottom-billion countries into the natural resource trap than to save them through export diversification.

Capital Flows and the Bottom Billion

The economies of the bottom billion are short of capital. Traditionally, aid has been supposed to supply the capital that the bottom billion lack, but even where this works it supplies only public capital, not private capital. Public capital can supply much of the infrastructure that these societies need, but it cannot begin to supply the equipment that workers need in order to be productive; that can be supplied only by private investors. As part of the work I describe below, we have measured the capital stock available for each member of the workforce, country by country. Africa is the most capital-scarce region, but this becomes dramatically more pronounced when capital is separated into its private and public components. In a successful region such as East Asia there is more than twice as much private capital as public capital. By contrast, Africa has twice as much public capital as private capital. What it and the other economies of the bottom billion really lack is private investment. This translates into a lack of equipment for the labor force to work with, and this in turn condemns workers to being unproductive and so to having low incomes. The labor force of the bottom billion needs private capital, and in principle globalization can provide it. Basic economic theory would suggest that in the societies that are short of capital, the returns on capital would be high, and this would attract an inflow of private capital.

Private Capital Inflows

Global capitalism does often work like this. China, for example, is attracting huge private capital inflows. Of course, the East Asian crisis of 1998, during which foreign money panicked and fled the region, showed that short-term financial inflows can be a mixed blessing, exposing countries to financial shocks. But longer-term investment is likely to be beneficial all around. Workers in developing countries get jobs and increased wages, and the firms that move capital to developing countries get higher returns on it. Such capital movements, like trade, normally generate mutual gains. Since political contests are usually presented as zero-sum games—your gain is my loss—the people who are most politically engaged have the hardest time believing in mutual gains. Hence, perhaps, the exaggerated suspicions of globalization.

But what about the bottom billion? Again, I think that the effect of globalization—this time through capital flows—is different. The biggest capital flows are not going to the countries that are most short of capital; they are bypassing the bottom billion. The top of the league for investment inflows has been Malaysia, a highly successful middle-income country. The only substantial inflows of private investment to the bottom billion have been to finance the extraction of natural resources—the top of the league among the bottom billion has been Angola, due to the opportunities for offshore oil.

Why are the most capital-scarce countries not attracting a larger capital inflow? Historically, part of the answer has been poor governance and policy. Obviously, this does not impede capital inflows for resource extraction—hence Angola—but it has curtailed the footloose investment in manufacturing, services, and agribusiness. Since the 1990s quite a few of the societies of the bottom billion have implemented significant reforms of governance and policies. The problem is that even these reforming countries are not attracting significant inflows of private capital. The key question is why not. To try to answer it I teamed up with Cathy Pattillo, an African American now working at the IMF.

The answer is that the perceived risk of investment in the economies of the bottom billion remains high. Investor perceptions of risk can be measured—one useful indicator is a survey, done by the magazine

Institutional Investor, that scores the perceived risk for each country on a scale of 1 to 100. A score of 100 implies the sort of maximum safety appropriate for your grandmother's nest egg, and a score of 1 is only for kamikaze investors. Risk ratings such as this one show up as significant in statistical explanations of private investment; unsurprisingly, high risk discourages investment.

The problem for the reforming countries of the bottom billion is that the risk ratings take a long time to reflect turnarounds. I first came across this problem when I was advising the reforming government of Uganda in the early 1990s. The government had taken some remarkably brave decisions, and the economy was starting on what was to prove a prolonged period of rapid growth. At that time the *Institutional Investor* rating gave Uganda 5 out of 100, the worst rating in Africa. This was so far out of line with what the government was doing that it was worth mounting an image-building campaign with investors. Gradually, the ratings improved. I remember bumping into the Ugandan economic team at a meeting in Hong Kong in 1997. The latest issue of *Institutional Investor* had just come out, and they rushed up to me in excitement, saying, "Have you seen it?" They had achieved one of the largest improvements in the world, with their score rising from 18 to 23—but it was still well below the level at which serious investment inflows were likely, which is about 30 to 40. Why does it take so long for investors to revise their views of the bottom billion? There are three reasons for the problem.

Paradoxically, the countries with the strongest reforms are those that started from the worst governance and policies. Often things have to get really bad to provoke incisive change. And so the reforms start from a truly terrible rating, much as happened in Uganda. If you start from 5, it is going to take a while before you get to the range at which investment flows set in.

The second problem is that the typical economy of the bottom billion is very small. A corollary is that the community of private investors knows virtually nothing about it—absorbing information is costly, if only in time, and these places are simply not sufficiently important enough to bother with. This became evident when the government of Uganda was trying to change the country's image. The last time Uganda had been in the news had been because of Idi Amin, the publicity-obsessed coup leader who, not content with being styled president, had also made himself a field marshal (or to give him his fuller title, His Excellency, President for Life, Field Marshal Al Hadji Dr. Idi Amin, VC, DSO, MC, Lord of All the Beasts of the Earth and Fishes of the Sea, and Conqueror of the British Empire in Africa in General and Uganda in Particular). By the early 1990s Amin had been gone for over a decade, but most potential investors still thought he was president. There are fifty-eight countries in the bottom billion, and investors do not track them individually but think of them collectively as "Africa" and dismiss them. Contrast this with China: every major international company knows that it has to keep abreast of developments in China. This even shows up statistically: one team of researchers has shown that the investor ratings systematically exaggerate the problems of the countries of the bottom billion.

The third reason is that policy improvements are often genuinely fairly fragile: many incipient turnarounds subsequently abort. Reform is always politically difficult and, as we will see in the next chapter, it has not been helped by donor policy conditionality. Even the governments that genuinely want to reform are usually pushed into the role of opposing some of the reforms urged on them by the donors, because the donors want everything to happen at once. And governments that do not want to reform periodically take the money, embark on a few reforms, and then abandon them. So the genuine reformers have not been able to distinguish themselves from the bogus reformers. Because they cannot distinguish themselves, investors lump them all together and say, "Don't call us, we'll call you." They go to China instead.

Fundamentally, the problem is one of credibility. Reforms induced by donor money are not credible with investors, and even without donor money they are high-risk. What can a government that is genuinely committed to reform do about it? Economic theory does give us the right answer, but it is not very attractive. The government needs to create a convincing signal of its intentions, and to do this it has to adopt reforms that are so painful that a bogus reformer is simply not prepared to adopt them. It thereby reveals its true type, to use the language of economics. The Ugandan government actually did this. It restored property to its rightful owners, the Asians who had been expelled by Amin. In the run-up to a presidential election the Ugandan government also slashed the size of the civil service, throwing thousands out of work. Such decisions raised its risk rating so sharply. Though necessary to change investor perceptions, this signaling strategy both is harsh and runs the risk of creating a political backlash. In Part 4, I am going to discuss ways in which credibility might be achieved less painfully.

Private Capital Outflows

The lack of capital inflows is only half the story of why global capital markets are not working for the bottom billion. The other half is that their own capital flows out of them. Much of this is illegal, and so it is hidden. It is called capital flight. To find out whether capital is flowing out of the bottom billion you need to get under the skin of the official numbers. This was a big task, and it took three of us to crack it: I joined forces with both Cathy Pattillo and Anke Hoeffler, and it took us a very long time.

Suppose you live in a bottom-billion country and want to get your money out. You have to get hold of foreign currency—dollars. It's often illegal; in many cases all foreign currency has to be sold to the central bank at the official exchange rate, so what can you do? There are various tricks, one of which is to falsify the documentation on exports. You find someone who is exporting $1,000 worth of coffee to the United States. That individual bribes a few people in the customs office so that the documentation says $500. This way, the exporter only has to hand over $500 to the central bank. He can then sell the other $500 to you, and you can deposit it in a foreign bank. To find evidence of such schemes, we looked for discrepancies in the numbers—the coffee exporter bribes the local customs officers but not the American customs officials, so the documentation at the U.S. end of the transaction correctly records that $1,000 worth of coffee has been imported into the United States. By comparing export figures with import figures and using other discrepancies, it is possible to tease out capital flight year by year for each country. This allows you to discover, for example, that by the end of military rule in Nigeria in 1998 Nigerians were holding around $100 billion of capital outside the country. It became a newspaper sensation when I reported it to the annual conference of the Central Bank of Nigeria in Abuja.

We then estimated the value of private wealth held in each country, year by year. This may sound difficult, but you can work it out from data on private investment using something called the "perpetual inventory method." Finally, we added the private wealth held as capital flight abroad to the private wealth held within the country, to see what proportion of total private wealth was held abroad. This yielded what rapidly became one of the famous numbers about Africa: By 1990, 38 percent of its private wealth was held abroad. This was a greater proportion than in any other region. It was even higher than the Middle East, where oil wealth and deserts, unsurprisingly, tend to encourage investment abroad. Africa integrated into the global financial economy, but in the wrong direction: the most capital-scarce region in the world exported its capital. (As can be surmised from my description of how we arrived at that 38 percent figure, the technique is not precise. We can reliably say that capital flight has been substantial, but quite how big we do not really know.)

So Africans were voting with their wallets, taking their money out of the region. What was driving this massive capital flight? If you ask Africans, they tell you it is corruption. Those in power loot public money and get it safely abroad. This is surely part of the story, but it is not at the heart of what is going on. For example, Indonesia had corruption on a world-class scale. President Suharto took what we might politely term "Asian family values" to extraordinary heights of paternalistic generosity. But most of the money stayed in the country. Africans took their money, whether corruptly acquired or honestly acquired, out of Africa because the opportunities for investment were so poor. One reason why the investment opportunities were so poor was because the countries were stuck in one or another of the traps. Capital flight was a response to the traps. In the sophisticated language of professional economics, capital flight was a "portfolio choice": people were holding their assets where they would yield a reasonable and a safe return. How do we know? We tried to explain the portfolio choices statistically. Why, for example, did Indonesians in 1980 hold nearly all their wealth domestically, whereas Ugandans in 1986 held two-thirds of their wealth abroad? We tried a whole range of explanations, such as measures of corruption and measures of the returns on capital. We found that in addition to the problem that the traps depressed the returns on capital, investment opportunities were judged poor because of the perceived high level of risk, as measured by means of indices such as the *Institutional*

Investor ratings described above. The credibility problem was not just scaring off foreigners—it was scaring off domestic investors as well.

So, despite being chronically short of private capital, the bottom billion are integrating into the global economy through capital flight rather than capital inflows. They are losing capital partly because the traps involve conditions such as political instability and poor policies, which make countries unsuited for investment. But even when countries succeed in shedding these characteristics they are still perceived as risky, and fears of retrogression keep capital out. So don't count on global capital mobility to develop the bottom billion, capital-scarce as they are. It is more likely to reinforce the traps.

Migration and the Bottom Billion

The bottom billion have not only integrated into the world economy through capital flight. They are increasingly integrating through migration. People vote with their feet as well as with their wallets. Historically, migration has been the great equalizer. In the nineteenth century the vast movement of people from Europe to North America did more to raise and equalize incomes than trade or capital movements. And more recently for some developing countries, migration has been a very good thing. For example, the Indian diaspora in the United States was probably critical in India's breakthrough into the world market for e-services. For those bottom-billion countries with the least favorable prospects, migration offers a safety valve; as I discussed in Chapter 4, it is one strategy for countries such as Niger. But how does it look more generally for the bottom billion?

Having studied capital flight, Cathy, Anke, and I decided to try a similar approach with migration. We distinguished between the educated and the uneducated. With a bit of imagination you can think of education as a form of wealth: in one of the ugliest phrases in economics, educated people are "human capital," so labeled because their skills are valuable. We wondered whether the migration behavior of the educated from developing countries looked more like that of uneducated people or more like the portfolio choices of capital. I have to say I rather hoped that the educated would look more like people than like portfolios, that all the myriad features that humanity holds in common would swamp the value that the educated and portfolios have in common. But it was not to be. The migration decisions of educated people looked very like the portfolio decisions that determine where wealth is held, and not much at all like the migration decisions of the uneducated, who are more likely to migrate the wider the differential between their earnings at home and what they can earn abroad.

What does this imply for the bottom billion? It suggests that these countries will hemorrhage their educated people to a far greater extent than their uneducated people. Migration takes time to build up, but it accelerates. There is a simple reason for this: migration becomes easier if other family members have already moved. Our analysis predicts that the exodus of capital from the bottom billion was only phase one of the global integration of the bottom billion. Phase two will be an exodus of educated people. As Somalia continues to fail and other places continue to develop, more Somalis will leave, as there will be more places for them to go. But emigration will be selective: the brightest and the best will have most to gain from moving. They are also the ones most likely to be welcomed in host countries. Ordinary Somalis will have less incentive to leave because they lack the skills to gain employment, and indeed, they will become increasingly unwelcome and so will find it harder to leave Somalia. Those who do get out will not return, and their remittances will dwindle after a generation of separation. Emigration helps those who leave, but it can have perverse effects on those left behind, especially if it selectively removes the educated. Yet this is precisely what we predict: having already hemorrhaged capital, the countries at the bottom will increasingly hemorrhage educated labor—people like my friend Lemma Sembet, an Ethiopian who is one of America's leading professors of finance. Meanwhile, back in the countries of the bottom billion, the financial sectors are run by people whose understanding of financial economics does not equip them to manage much more than a piggy bank.

Remember from Chapter 5 that to achieve a turnaround from being a failing state, a country is helped by having a critical mass of educated people. The countries of the bottom billion are already desperately short of qualified people, and the situation is likely to get worse. The flight of the skilled is at its most rapid in precisely those bottom-billion environments where there is most scope for change: postconflict societies. So, whereas migration has generally been helpful as part of the development process, I am skeptical of it as a force for transforming the bottom billion. I think that by draining these countries of their talent, migration is more likely to make it harder for these nations to decisively escape the trap of bad policy and governance.

Life in Limbo: Out of the Frying Pan . . .

This all adds up to a depressing picture of what globalization is doing for the bottom billion. To get a chance to play in the global economy, you need to break free of the traps, and that is not easy. Remember, in order to turn a country around it helps to have a pool of educated people, but the global labor market is draining the bottom billion of their limited pool of such people. Even once they reform, many of these economies find it difficult to attract private investment inflows, and may continue to hemorrhage their own modest private wealth. And they face a high hurdle in trying to break into diversified markets for exports because China, India, and the other successful developing countries have already done so. Even once free of the traps, countries are liable to be stuck in a kind of limbo—no longer falling apart, but not able to replicate the rapid growth of Asia, and so failing to converge.

This indeed seems to describe a lot of bottom-billion countries that have recently come out of the traps. Remember that in the past four years the average country of the bottom billion has at last started to grow. I have interpreted that as a temporary phenomenon linked to the global boom in commodities. But suppose you were to put the most favorable gloss on it—that they have broken free of the traps. Well, although they are growing, it is at a very sedate pace—much more slowly than the other developing countries even during the slow decade of the 1970s. Even if their present growth rate is sustained, they will continue to diverge rapidly. It will take them many decades to reach what we now consider to be the threshold of middle income, and by that time the rest of the world will have moved on.

There is also a yet more depressing variant of the future for these limbo countries: the traps still await them. As long as they have low incomes and slow growth they continue to play Russian roulette. Côte d'Ivoire survived low income and slow growth for a couple of decades but then fell into conflict as the result of a coup. Zimbabwe survived the same and then fell into bad governance. Tanzania, currently among the most hopeful low-income countries, is about to become resource-rich due to new discoveries of gas and gold. Malawi grew remarkably well for the first decade of its independence, considering that is landlocked and resource-scarce, but then its neighbors fell into the conflict trap and, being dependent upon them, it too began to decline. And so a miserable but possible scenario is that countries in the bottom billion oscillate between the traps and limbo, perhaps switching in the process from one trap to another.

In the next part of the book we will at last turn from the depressing scenarios of traps and limbos to what we can do about them. Let me be clear: *we* cannot rescue *them*. The societies of the bottom billion can only be rescued from within. In every society of the bottom billion there are people working for change, but usually they are defeated by the powerful internal forces stacked against them. We should be helping the heroes. So far, our efforts have been paltry: through inertia, ignorance, and incompetence, we have stood by and watched them lose.

Part 4

The Instruments

CHAPTER 7

Aid to the Rescue?

THE STORY SO FAR: a group of countries with nearly a billion people living in them have been caught in one or another of four traps. As a result, while the rest of the developing world has been growing at an unprecedented rate, they have stagnated or even declined. From time to time they have broken free of the traps, but the global economy is now making it much harder for them to follow the path taken by the more successful majority. As a result, even when free of the traps they sit in limbo, growing so slowly that they risk falling back into the traps before they can reach a level of income that ensures safety.

A future world with a billion people living in impoverished and stagnant countries is just not a scenario we can countenance. A cesspool of misery next to a world of growing prosperity is both terrible for those in the cesspool and dangerous for those who live next to it. We had better do something about it. The question is what. This chapter and the ones that follow answer that question. I start with aid—the stuff of rock bands, G8 promises, and agencies—but I do not stop there. Aid alone is really unlikely, in my view, to be able to address the problems of the bottom billion, and it has become so highly politicized that its design is often pretty dysfunctional. Therefore I move on to three other instruments that would, I think, be effective but have been grossly underused to date.

What is it about aid that causes such intense political disagreements? It seems to bring out the worst in both left and right. The left seems to want to regard aid as some sort of reparations for colonialism. In other words, it's a statement about the guilt of Western society, not about development. In this view, the only role for the bottom billion is as victims: they all suffer from our sins. The right seems to want to equate aid with welfare scrounging. In other words, it is rewarding the feckless and so accentuating the problem. Between these two there is a thin sliver of sanity called aid for development. It runs something like this: We used to be that poor once. It took us two hundred years to get to where we are. Let's try to speed things up for these countries.

Aid does tend to speed up the growth process. A reasonable estimate is that over the last thirty years it has added around one percentage point to the annual growth rate of the bottom billion. This does not sound like a whole lot, but then the growth rate of the bottom billion over this period has been much less than 1 percent per year—in fact, it has been zero. So adding 1 percent has made the difference between stagnation and severe cumulative decline. Without aid, cumulatively the countries of the bottom billion would have become much poorer than they are today. Aid has been a holding operation preventing things from falling apart.

In July 2005 at Gleneagles, the G8 summit committed to doubling aid to Africa. Is this going to double the contribution of aid to growth? Is it going to drag the bottom billion out of stagnation? If by doubling it you could add another percentage point to growth, the effect, while not dramatic, would at least gradually cumulate to substantially higher incomes. I think that with the right complementary changes this might happen, but as things currently stand, additional aid will not have such promising results. The statistical evidence generally suggests that aid is subject to what is called "diminishing returns." That is, as you keep on increasing aid, you get less and less bang for the buck: the first million dollars is more productive than the second, and so on. This is not very surprising, as diminishing returns are found all over the place and it would be odd if aid escaped. A recent study by the Center for Global Development, a Washington think tank, came up with an estimate of diminishing returns implying that when aid reaches about 16 percent of GDP it more or less ceases to be effective. Africa wasn't far off that level even before Gleneagles. So with the doubling of aid, if indeed it happens, we have broadly reached the limits to aid absorption, at least under existing modalities.

Can we change the way aid is provided, to make it more effective and increase the scope for aid absorption? There are plenty of horror stories about aid bureaucracies. Donors often trip over each other and fail to co-ordinate. I came across one case where three donor agencies each wanted to build a hospital in the same place. They agreed to coordinate, which doesn't always happen, but then faced the problem of having three in-compatible sets of rules for how the work should be commissioned. It took them two years to reach a compromise, which was that each agency should build one floor of the hospital under its own rules. You can imag-ine how efficient that was likely to be. So there is plenty of room for im-provement on the ground. Agencies also impose their own complex and differing accounting procedures upon recipient governments that have very limited capacity to manage even their own budgets, let alone those of donors. All this could indeed be made a whole lot simpler. The simplest is something called "budget support," which basically means that the donors give the government the money and it spends it on whatever it chooses, as if it were its own tax revenue. Aid just supports the budget. In some situ-ations this is the best way to transfer aid, but it depends upon the budget being reasonable. In many countries of the bottom billion the budget is not reasonable, and in some it is grotesque.

The world has already conducted a natural experiment in giving the countries of the bottom billion a huge injection of budget support. It is called oil. Recall from Chapter 3 that a number of bottom-billion countries have received large inflows of oil revenue, much of which must have reached the budget. For example, over the last thirty years Nigeria has re-ceived something on the order of $280 billion. This is far larger than any realistic scale of aid to a bottom-billion country. Yet Nigeria has depress-ingly little to show for it. That was the past, however; how about now? The recent increase in oil prices provides a natural experiment about as current as we can get. Africa's oil-exporting economies have between them recently received a bonanza that dwarfs feasible increases in aid. So I looked to see what this had done for the non-oil part of their economies, and compared it to the growth of the rest of Africa, which, not having oil, of course got hit by these high oil prices. The latest data I could get from the IMF are for 2004. Adding them up, I found that the two growth rates were identical: those economies that were benefiting from the oil windfall were growing no faster than the ones that were hit by it. Let us hope that this is just a matter of lags and that the oil economies will soon surge ahead. But so far, recent evidence is pretty consistent with past evidence: large inflows of money without any restrictions do not seem to be well spent in many of the countries of the bottom billion. In effect, budget support turns aid into oil: money for the governments of the bottom billion without restrictions on its use. So, to a first approximation, does debt relief. I am not against budget support and debt relief; they surely make sense for some countries. But as general instruments for developing the bottom billion they would be more reassuring had oil and other natural resource revenues been more successful.

Overall, despite the bureaucracy, aid has been much more successful than oil. Aid has raised growth, oil has lowered it. Yet both are financial transfers to bottom billion governments. The only difference is that aid has been handled by the aid agencies. So, unlikely as it seems, what the aid agencies have been doing has added a whole lot of value to the financial transfer. Given the bad public image of aid agencies and horror stories such as the hospital project I described above, this is hard to believe, but there it is. The projects, procedures, conditions, and suchlike have been beneficial overall, enhancing the value of the money transferred compared with just sending a check and hoping for the best. So getting rid of all this and just sending the money is more likely to make aid less effective than to make it more so. There are things we can do, and I will come to them, but the simple answer of just giving them the money is likely to be the right one only in the better-governed countries.

Aid has tended to be more effective where governance and policies are already reasonable. That does not sound very surprising: indeed, it sounds almost platitudinous. But it is actually pretty controversial. Partly, people quite reasonably do not like the harsh-sounding implication that the countries with the worst problems should get the least money. They obviously have the greatest need. However, there comes a point at which money is pretty ineffective in these environments. Recall that expenditure tracking survey in Chad: less than 1 percent of the money released by the Ministry of Finance for rural health clinics actually reached the clinics. In 2005 the European Commission gave 20 million euros to the government of Chad in budget support. How much of it do you imagine was well spent? Do not forget that the tracking survey was only following money that was already intended for health care. This is not, unfortunately, a very high priority for the government of Chad. It prefers to spend its money on the military. The budget support given by the European Union can be spent on whatever the government chooses. I doubt whether much of it was allocated to health. And of the money allocated to health, we know how much actually reaches the front line of health care. So the European Commission's well-intentioned support for the desperately poor country of Chad is likely to have ended up largely financing the army.

Is this the fate of aid in general? Donors try pretty hard to avoid inadvertently financing military spending, but what do the data show about how much aid leaks into military budgets? It was not easy to determine this, not least because the data on military spending are not very reliable. Governments tend to be, shall we say, economical with the truth. Anke Hoeffler and I relied upon the Stockholm Peace Research Institute for the data. The institute would be the first to admit that the data have problems, but they are probably the best available (believe it or not, even the data on aid are inadequate—you would think that donors could keep better track of how much they give to whom and in what form). Anyway, after the data came the problem of interpreting causation: it runs in both directions, with aid affecting military spending and military spending affecting aid. That is, donor behavior is purposive: governments with high levels of military spending tend to get less aid. We allowed for this. Our conclusion was that some aid does indeed leak into military spending, but surprisingly little—our best estimate is about 11 percent. This is not negligible, but on the basis of this it would be grossly unfair to claim that aid is wasted. Nevertheless, in those bottom-billion societies that get a lot of aid, even 11 percent of it adds up to quite a lot of the military budget. We estimate that something around 40 percent of Africa's military spending is inadvertently financed by aid. So the donors have a legitimate interest in restraining military spending, or at least in worrying about it.

To be fair, the aid agencies are in something of a bind. If they allocate aid only according to need, it ends up financing the army in Chad. If they allocate it only according to effectiveness in the growth process, it ends up going to those with less need. Together with David Dollar, my colleague at the World Bank, I came up with the idea that aid should be allocated so as to lift as many people out of poverty as possible. We tried to see how, in practice, need and effectiveness could be reconciled. In deference to the technocratic mind-set we termed our idea "poverty efficiency" (which must rank with "human capital" as a linguistic carbuncle). Anyway, the actual allocation of aid was very far from being poverty-efficient. The biggest deviation was that far too much aid was going to middle-income countries rather than to the bottom billion. The middle-income countries get aid because they are of much more commercial and political interest than the tiny markets and powerlessness of the bottom billion. Not all agencies are equally guilty. If we take the two biggest, the World Bank is far better protected from political influence than the European Commission, and so its aid has been much better targeted to the poorest countries. But herein lies a paradox: the World Bank until very recently has only been able to provide loans, whereas aid from the European Commission is entirely in the form of grants. So the loans have been going to the poorest countries and the grants to the middle-income countries. You might reasonably think that this is not particularly sensible and that aid allocation could be greatly improved. But if aid were better targeted to the bottom billion, would it help break the traps?

Aid and the Conflict Trap

Can aid actually make things worse? Some researchers think so: aid may be an inducement to rebellion and to coups because capturing the state becomes more valuable. In the societies of the bottom billion, aid is probably the key part of what is sometimes called the "rents to sovereignty"—the payoff to power. So is big aid an incentive to rebellion or to coups? How do you tell—conduct a survey of rebels and coup leaders?

Anke and I followed the same general method for both rebellions and coups: look at all of them and try to allow for the fact that aid is allocated purposively, so less tends to go to countries with the highest risks. Then, allowing for this purposive allocation, bring aid into the analysis of the causes of rebellion and the causes of coups. Of course, with this approach you cannot tell whether aid has had an effect in any particular instance, but you can tell whether it has a significant effect overall.

On average, as far as we can tell, aid has no direct effect on the risk of civil war, though it has indirect effects (which I will come to shortly). This does not mean that it never has direct effects: people expert in particular situations can give you stories on each side, of aid inciting war or averting it. Any of these may well be right, but they do not add up to a systematic relationship. With coups it is a different matter: big aid indeed makes a coup more likely. So, going back to some of the results of Chapter 2, rebellions are encouraged by natural resource wealth but not by aid, and coups are encouraged by aid. Why this difference? Perhaps, because a rebellion usually takes many years, the prospect of aid if the state is eventually captured is not a potent lure. Resource rents, by contrast, are useful to rebels in the here and now of the conflict because they can be grabbed along the way; you don't need to control the entire state to control a diamond mine in the middle of nowhere. And why is aid a lure to coups if it isn't to rebellions? Perhaps because a coup does not take many years before it is resolved. It is over virtually as soon as it has begun, and if it is successful, the aid is there for the taking.

So to an extent aid does make the conflict trap worse. But it can also make things better. Recall that the key risk factors in rebellions and coups are slow growth and low income. The indirect effects of aid on conflict risk are benign. By raising growth and thereby cumulatively raising income, aid reduces these risks. Is the payoff worth the costs? Anke and I tried to answer that question. We already had an estimate of the costs of the typical civil war—around $64 billion—and we had just estimated how aid would reduce the risk of war through raising growth. So by putting the two together we got an estimate of the payoff to aid from enhanced security. To our surprise, it turned out that the payoff was not big enough to justify the cost. The reason was that aid was not very effective at raising growth in the conditions of poor governance and policies that typified the bottom billion. Challenged by Jeff Sachs, who thought we had asked the right question but come up with the wrong answer, we experimented. In countries with better governance and policies—that is, the countries that had already broken free of the poor governance trap—the security benefits started to mount up, reaching perhaps half of the cost of the aid. And of course our cost of conflict did not include any adverse spillovers for rich countries, such as drugs and terrorism. So although security considerations alone probably do not justify a big aid program, in some countries they are a substantial addition to the normal benefits of aid—higher income and increased domestic consumption.

However, the cost-benefit analysis of aid for security looks very different in postconflict situations. In these situations the security benefits alone are more than enough to justify a large aid program. Recall that these are the times of highest risk—around half of all civil wars are postconflict situations gone wrong. Aid happens to be particularly effective in raising the growth rate in these situations. This is hardly surprising—this is how aid got started. The World Bank was originally called the International Bank for Reconstruction and Development, and in fact the "and Development" bit was literally an add-on. Aid was invented to rebuild Europe after the Second World War. It worked. In more recent times the mistake with aid to postconflict situations has been that it has been too little and too soon. Yes, too *soon*. The peace settlements hit the media and the politicians hit their checkbooks. Aid floods in during the first couple of years, then rapidly dries up. Yet the typical postconflict country starts with truly terrible governance, institutions, and policies. It takes some time to improve them to a level at which aid can be of much use. So big aid needs to be sustained during the first decade postconflict, not just the first couple of years. To their credit, the donors are learning. Postconflict interventions really got going only after the end of the Cold War—until then, everything was too polarized. So the stock of experience has been pretty limited. For example, the World Bank introduced postconflict considerations into its criteria for aid allocation only around 2000—in the years of the Cold War its reconstruction role had been forgotten. And even when it introduced its special postconflict allocation, the extra money for a country was designed to be phased out after the first three years. In 2005 the rules were changed so that the extra money now lasts for seven years, a much more reasonable time frame. Agencies are learning, and aid so used has an important role to play in breaking the conflict trap. But aid alone is not enough. Growth is a slow process, and it takes time to bring risks down. After a decade of rapid growth, postconflict risks are usually brought down to manageable levels. But during that first decade, even big aid cannot do much to bring the risks down. We have to look at other ways of containing risks during that period while aid does its slow work of rebuilding the economy.

Other than in the postconflict period, to the extent that aid raises growth it is also useful in bringing down the risk of conflict. But the problem is designing aid in such a way that it works even in the environments of poor governance and poor policy that are most at risk of conflict. I will come to that. Let's first look at how aid affects the other traps.

Aid and the Natural Resource Trap

The second trap was the natural resource trap. Here, frankly, aid is fairly impotent. Evidently, the resource-rich countries have money coming into the government. They do not use it very well. There is nevertheless a moment for aid in these environments. That moment is when they try to reform—an incipient turnaround. I will return to it in the discussion of the trap of poor governance and policy.

Aid and the Trap of Being Landlocked

The third trap was being landlocked. These are the countries that basically need to be on international welfare for a long time. Eventually they might become viable, depending upon when their more fortunate neighbors start to grow and what market niches turn up. But we should not pretend that there are easy answers. In the meantime, there is no fast track available for these countries. In retrospect, it was perhaps a mistake for the international system to permit economically unviable areas to become independent countries. But the deed is done, and we have to live with the consequences. One of the consequences is the need for big aid as a means of raising domestic consumption in these desperately poor environments, even if the aid does not do much for growth. For these countries the psychology of aid needs to recognize that it is not there as a temporary stimulus to development, it is there to bring some minimal decency to standards of living.

Probably the key role for development aid—as opposed to direct support for consumption—in the landlocked countries is to improve their transport links to the coasts. Recall that the costs of transport to the coast vary enormously and tend to reflect the transport infrastructure of neighbors. Aid should have been financing the regional transport corridors that are the lifelines for the landlocked. It has largely failed to do so. Why?

One reason was that in the 1990s infrastructure went out of fashion, at least for aid agencies. This was partly because there was an exaggerated belief that the private sector would finance infrastructure, so the aid agencies had better find something else to justify their continued existence. For example, in the World Bank, an agency whose core business had been infrastructure, infrastructure was now lumped in with private-sector development and finance, the whole package being merely one of five "networks." The shift away from infrastructure was also because there was growing pressure to spend aid on the photogenic social priorities—health and education—and on the increasingly sacred environmental goals (both of which got networks all to themselves at the World Bank). So agencies shifted their budgets away from infrastructure to make room for increased spending on the new priorities.

The other reason why regional transport corridors got neglected was that aid programs were overwhelmingly organized country by country. Uganda's link to the coast depended upon transport infrastructure in Kenya, not in Uganda. But the Kenyan government did not care about Uganda, and with the growing emphasis upon "country ownership" of aid programs, if the government of Kenya did not care then neither did those donors who gave money to Kenya. So the underfunding of infrastructure and country-driven aid programs together did in the regional transport corridors that the landlocked needed.

Aid and the Trap of Bad Governance

The fourth trap was being stuck with very poor governance and policies. Can aid help in getting countries out of these problems? This is where I think there is the most scope for additional aid. There are three ways in which aid can potentially help turnarounds: incentives, skills, and reinforcement. Let us see what works.

Aid as an Incentive

The use of aid as an incentive for policy improvement was initiated in the 1980s. It was known as policy conditionality. The donors provided aid if the government promised to reform. It was a pretty hopeless failure. There were two basic problems with it: the psychology and the economics. The psychological reaction to being told to do something is resistance. Any parent knows that, and it is just as true of governments as it is of children; how else can they establish their freedom? So conditionality pushed governments, and indeed whole societies, into opposing policy changes that would have been highly beneficial. Policy conditionality also messed up accountability. If governments were being ordered about by donor agencies, whom should an electorate blame if things went wrong? Governments were quick to exploit the full potential for evading responsibility. In the week when the government of Zimbabwe launched economic reforms in 1998, its minister of information told the local press, "They're not our reforms, they're the IMF's. We had to do them." That sort of statement not only shifted the responsibility but made the reforms very easy to reverse. And the government of Zimbabwe most surely reversed them.

Policy conditionality as then practiced depended upon the government promising to make changes. This, for those of you who prefer to think in Latin, is known as ex ante conditionality. The economics of getting money on the basis of a promise is known as the time consistency problem. Unless incentives are properly aligned, governments will promise, take the money, and then do what they like. To give you a real-life example, the government of Kenya promised the same reform to the World Bank in return for aid five times over a fifteen-year period. Yes, five times it took the money and either did nothing or made token reforms that it then reversed. The amazing thing is that the money kept coming. How did Kenyan government officials manage to keep straight, sincere faces as for the fifth time they made the same commitment? How did officials of the agency manage to delude themselves into thinking that adherence this time was likely? But aid agencies have very little incentive to enforce conditions: people get promoted by disbursing money, not by withholding it. Eventually, the World Bank and other donor agencies realized this limitation and largely switched to disbursing aid on the basis of the attained level of policies rather than on promises of improvement. For the Latin-speakers, this is ex post conditionality. It was more consistent with the research evidence that suggested that whether aid worked well depended upon the level of policies rather than on how they were changing, and it avoided the need for promises. The only problem was that it squeezed aid out of the very countries that have the biggest problems. On the most favorable interpretation, it was a realistic recognition of the limits of aid to help in these environments. On a less favorable interpretation, it was giving up on the very environments where the agencies were most needed. Anyway, forget ex ante policy conditionality as a way of inducing policy improvement in failing states: it just doesn't work.

I take a very different view of *governance* conditionality. The key objective of governance conditionality is not to shift power from governments to donors but to shift power from governments to their own citizens. The struggle for this transfer of power took around two hundred years in Europe, and we should indeed want to speed it up in the bottom billion. External pressure was vital in the European struggle. The most common account of that struggle goes as follows. The threat of war forced governments to defend themselves with big armies. To pay for these armies the governments needed to tax. To get compliance for high taxation they had to concede representation and scrutiny. We cannot go through that process in the bottom billion. In Europe the threat of war turned into a reality sufficiently often for the whole process to have been murderous, and it would probably be so again. It was also slow. But the purely internal processes by which citizens force governments to accept scrutiny are probably pretty weak. External pressure is needed. And it is entirely legitimate. Why should we give aid to governments that are not willing to let their citizens see how they spend it?

Governance conditionality, in its ex post form, is gaining in popularity. Most dramatically, U.S. president George W. Bush launched his new Millennium Challenge Account based largely on allocation criteria of attained levels of governance. He wisely chose not to allocate the additional American aid money through the established American aid agency, for over the years USAID has been captured by congressional commercial lobbies. Voting line by line on USAID's budget, Congress has diverted spending so as to benefit particular American exporters, unrelated to African needs. However, somewhat surprisingly, no agency is doing ex ante governance conditionality. One advantage of such an approach is that it would be much clearer what a government had to do, and on what time scale, in order to be rewarded by extra aid. And the aid could be targeted to countries that initially had weak governance—so it would focus on the bottom billion instead of excluding them. I will spell out more fully what I think could be the practical content of governance conditionality in Part 5. We have to accept that there are severe limits to what aid can do to improve governance. But we are not yet at those limits.

Aid as Skills

Conditionality looms large in discussions of aid because it is so sensitive, but reform of governance and policies is not just a matter of political will and political pressure. It also requires people with the relevant skills. Typically, in the societies of the bottom billion the civil service has lost whatever skills it once possessed. Once over dinner the former head of the civil service in one of the big bottom-billion societies described what had happened to the civil service that he had helped to build. He asked me to imagine being a schoolboy in his country on the eve of independence. The bright boys in the class aspired to join the civil service to help build the country. At the other end of the class, what were the aspirations for the dumb class bully? Forget the civil service with its tough exam. So the class bully set his sights on the army. Fast-forward two decades and a coup d'état. The army was now running the government. Between the class bullies, now the generals, and their objective of looting the public sector stood the class stars now running the civil service. The generals didn't like it. Gradually they replaced the clever boys with people more like themselves. And as they promoted the dumb and corrupt over the bright and the honest, the good chose to leave. Economists have a term for it: "selection by intrinsic motivation." So by the time the military ceded power back to civilian politicians, the civil service was broken: far from being the vehicle for developing the country, it was a vehicle for looting it.

Politics is full of idiosyncrasies, and from time to time reform-minded ministers and presidents come to power. But it is very difficult for them to implement change because they inherit a civil service that is an obstacle rather than an instrument. It is hostile to change because individual civil servants profit from the tangled mess of regulations and expenditures over which they preside. Aid has a potential role of providing the skills that the civil service lacks when they are most needed.

Recall from Chapter 5 that together with Lisa Chauvet I looked at the preconditions for a turnaround from a failing state and for the conditions that helped success once a turnaround had started. In fact, the main purpose of our work was to see whether aid was helpful, either as a precondition or once a turnaround had started. We decided to distinguish between two types of aid: technical assistance and money to governments. Technical assistance means the supply of skilled people, paid for by the donor. Although the donor spends money, what the recipient government gets are skilled foreigners to work for it. Technical assistance accounts for about a quarter of all the money spent on aid. The other three-quarters is money either handed to governments to finance specific projects such as a school or simply provided to the government without a specified use, which is called budget support. Even to distinguish between technical assistance and money to governments was difficult because the donor agencies just have not been bothered to record their activities properly. We relied upon data provided by the Paris-based Development Assistance Committee of the Organisation for Economic Co-operation and Development (OECD), the main donor club. Even they thought the data were of poor quality.

I am going to focus on technical assistance. Usually the fact that a quarter of aid is provided as technical assistance is presented as some sort of scandal, on the grounds that the countries do not see any money—all they get is people. But really it depends upon whether the people are of any use. Reforms need skills, and in the bottom billion these skills are lacking—remember, the skilled people have already left. They're in London, New York, and Paris, not Bangui. The politically correct answer to the need for technical assistance is to support "capacity building" instead: that means train the locals rather than fly in experts. There is a lot of sense in capacity building, but there is also a chicken-and-egg problem. Until the country has turned itself around, capacity building is pretty difficult. You train people to an international standard, and if there are no prospects, then they use their credentials as a passport out of the country. I know—I have been training people for three decades. In the early stages of reform not only do the reformers need skills that are unavailable in the country, but some of these skills will no longer be needed once the transition has been accomplished. It actually makes sense for a country to import a bunch of skills temporarily while it gets over the hump of reform.

So Lisa and I introduced technical assistance into our analysis of turnarounds. Did it help as a precondition for a turnaround? Did it help once a turnaround had already gotten started? Did it help when a new leader had just come to power? As usual with aid, we faced the problem that causality can run in both directions: the better the prospects of a turnaround, the more technical assistance the donors might choose to supply. To the extent that donors get this right, aid will tend to be targeted to situations that are ripe for improvement and hence subsequently do improve. With such behavior it is indeed likely that aid will appear to raise the chances of turnaround, but this would be because the wrong version of causality has been forced on the relationship. We might equally have found that a good prospect of reform causes aid to go up. The way to overcome the problem is to find a component of technical assistance that can be predicted country by country, year by year, and is devoid of any influence from the country's governance and policies. Fortunately, a substantial component of a country's aid receipts are determined not by its own current circumstances but by the characteristics of donors. For example, Ethiopia is likely to get a relatively large amount of aid from Italy, since Italians see their brief invasion of Ethiopia as giving them a historical connection. And Côte d'Ivoire is likely to get a relatively substantial amount of aid from France, its former colonial master (Abidjan used to be known as Africa's Paris). So if the Italian aid budget goes up and the French aid budget goes down, Ethiopia is likely to get an increase in its aid receipts relative to Côte d'Ivoire. Since this component of aid is unrelated to policy conditions in the recipient countries, we can study its effects on the chances of a turnaround and be fairly sure that causality is running only from aid to the turnaround. To continue the example, from time to time Ethiopia or Côte d'Ivoire gets lucky or unlucky with the configuration of aid donors, and we can see whether luck or the lack of it has any effect on the chances of turnaround.

Unfortunately, as far as we can tell, technical assistance in a failing state prior to turnaround has little effect on the prospect of a turnaround occurring. The experts come and preach and people listen politely, but not much happens. This is bad news for the agencies that do this and little else, and it is also bad news for failing states since pouring in big technical assistance would be pretty easy. However, things look dramatically different once a turnaround has started, or indeed if the state has a new leader.

Technical assistance during the first four years of an incipient reform, and especially during the first two years, has a big favorable effect on the chances that the momentum of the reforms will be maintained. It also substantially reduces the chance that the reforms will collapse altogether. To me this makes sense, because these early periods of turnaround are when the courage of a few brave politicians meets the brick wall of obduracy and incompetence in the civil service. Beyond the few reforms that just require the minister to sign something—stroke-of-the-pen reforms—most reform needs technocrats and managers able to implement change.

Lisa and I were quite surprised that the effect of technical assistance came out so strongly, and so we decided to push our luck. Could we tease out any sense of how much technical assistance was useful during this early phase of reform? Again to our surprise, we found that we got an answer in which we could have some statistical confidence. It told us that technical assistance packages during reform could usefully be really big—typically up to around $250 million a year could be spent on providing technical expertise before additional money became useless.

We first compared this with actual technical assistance during reform episodes. The actual scale of assistance was typically far lower, so donors appeared to be missing an opportunity. But at this stage we had not compared the costs with the benefits: if the benefits were sufficiently modest, then donors would be right in passing up these apparent opportunities. To discover whether pouring in technical assistance during incipient reforms is worth the money we needed to determine whether the benefits exceed the costs. It was simple enough because we already had our estimate of the costs of a failing state—around $100 billion—which I described in Chapter 5, and we now had the amount by which a technical assistance package would raise the chances of sustaining an incipient turnaround. We just had to bring the two together. The payoff came out at around $15 billion, and the cost of maximal technical assistance sustained for four years is only around $1 billion. So donors were in fact missing a really good opportunity for aid: spend $1 for an expected return of $15. And don't forget that the only benefits counted in that $100 billion are to the neighborhood; the additional security that spills over to the wider world is a bonus.

So why are aid agencies missing this opportunity? After all, it is not as if technical assistance overall were negligible—money spent on providing countries with the skilled people who constitute technical assistance is a quarter of total aid flows, so it is huge. The problem is not the overall insufficiency of technical assistance but rather that it is organized so as to be unresponsive to country circumstances. In the parlance of the agencies, technical assistance is supply-driven rather than demand-driven. The same assistance is poured into the same places year after year without much regard to political opportunities. Indeed, given the prevalence of ex post policy conditionality—putting the money where things are already satisfactory—agencies simply cannot put their resources into failing states early in a possible turnaround; it is against the rules. Technical assistance needs to be reorganized to look more like emergency relief and less like a pipeline of projects. Just as when the Southeast Asian tsunami struck in December 2004 emergency relief teams were quickly flown in, so when political opportunities arise, skills should be available. Ideally, reforming ministers need to be able to draw on a large technical assistance account, which is theirs to decide how to use. And this would be useful even in the resource-rich failing states. Although the governments of resource-rich countries have revenues that in principle could be used to pay for big technical assistance, they are unlikely to do so. The political cost of using revenues in that way at the start of a reform effort would be massive. And so, at the right time and for the right things, aid can be very productive even in breaking the natural resource trap.

Aid as Reinforcement

So aid as technical assistance can help turn around failing states. What about aid as money provided to the government intended for projects or budget support? We followed the same approach and got completely different results. Money early in reform is actually counterproductive. It makes it less likely that the reform will maintain momentum. I was pretty suspicious of this result until we found a completely separate result that looks remarkably similar. I briefly mentioned it in Chapter 5, but now I want to make more of it. This is the effect of terms of trade windfalls such as oil booms and coffee booms. You might imagine that an improvement in the terms of trade would make reform easier—after all, there is more money coming into the country and people are better off. It turns out to be the opposite, however: a terms-of-trade windfall early in a reform has the same adverse effect as an aid boom, in that early money chills the prospects of sustaining the reform. There is no technical economic reason for this, so it must be political. I wanted to get some insight as to whether the politics really was like this, so I asked Ngozi Okonjo-Iweala, who at the time was finance minister of Nigeria (and not just any finance minister, either—she was named Finance Minister of the Year for 2005 by *The Banker* in recognition of her efforts at reform). I first encountered her in the mid-1990s when she wrote to me at Oxford out of the blue. I was running a research center on African economies, and she was a director at the World Bank. She wrote asking whether she could come to the center for a month, using her vacation from the World Bank to study. Not many World Bank directors have done that. Anyway, by 2005 she was the ideal politician for this question: there she was, implementing reform, and doing it with remarkable success, in the midst of a huge oil boom. I asked her whether the high oil price that was generating big revenues for the Nigerian government was making reform easier or harder. She laughed. "Harder, much harder," was her assessment. Why? Because people's attention was focused on getting the extra oil money that they knew was there, rather than on the often painful, tedious, and fractious business of reform. Why lay off people when there is oil money? Why delay projects by insisting that the contracts be put out for competitive bid when there is money to pay in excess of the competitive price? And perhaps that is an example of a more general pattern: sudden extra money, whether from export booms or aid, detracts from the hard choices involved in reform.

After reform has continued for a few years, the statistical effects of technical assistance and money reverse themselves. Technical assistance becomes useless or even counterproductive—because, I suppose, governments at some stage need to build their own capacity, rather than continuing to rely upon outside experts—and money starts to become useful, reinforcing the reform process instead of undermining it. So what seems to show up is a sequence. Aid is not very effective in inducing a turnaround in a failing state; you have to wait for a political opportunity. When it arises, pour in the technical assistance as quickly as possible to help implement reform. Then, after a few years, start pouring in the money for the government to spend.

Aid used in this way to support incipient turnarounds would be pretty high-risk. Even with aid many incipient turnarounds would fail. The payoff is high because the successes, when they happen, are enormously valuable. The process of aiding turnarounds is thus analogous, in terms of risk taking, to a venture capital fund—most of the firms in which a venture capital fund invests fail, but the fund overall can be successful because of a few winners. For aid agencies to become truly focused on the bottom billion they will need to adapt to this high-risk mode of operation. The venture capital fund approach is, I think, the right managerial model for dealing with such risks because it reconciles accountability with incentives. A "venture aid fund" preserves accountability for overall performance, but managers can achieve overall success despite a lot of failures. Without this sort of model bureaucracies just cannot cope with risk. Their staff will not take large risks because they imply periodic failure, and failure means a blighted career. Unsurprisingly, people are simply not prepared to take risks on these terms. The situation is getting worse as people are increasingly assessed in terms of the "results" they achieve. Within aid agencies there is a vogue for a results orientation, and up to a point this is sensible—senior managers are trying to get their workforce to focus on outcomes, not inputs. But a focus on results can very easily encourage people to avoid failures at all costs. And if this happens aid will increasingly be directed to the safe option of countries where performance is already satisfactory. To its credit the British government has understood this problem and provided the World Bank with the money to launch a fund that can be used to support turnarounds. Will other governments put money into this fund? To my mind that is one of the critical steps for aid in the next couple of years. If you want your children to grow up in a world with fewer failing states, one of the practical things you can do about it is to urge your government to back this sort of aid finance.

Aid Prior to Reform

The effectiveness of money pre-turnaround depends upon how it is given. The traditional way of trying to ensure that aid is spent properly is through projects. Instead of just giving unencumbered money to the government, the agency agrees on a project with the government and helps to design and implement it. This is a cumbersome approach that is inappropriate for countries with reasonable governance, but for the countries with very weak governance it is probably sensible. There is, however, a catch: projects done in countries with weak governance and poor policies are known to be much more likely to fail.

Recently, Lisa and I were asked to investigate whether there was anything that could be done to make projects implemented in failing states more successful. The donors had liked our work on turnarounds enough to agree to finance a second phase. We used a huge data set that reported evaluations of thousands of donor projects around the world. It took us a long time to make sense of it, and I will issue a caveat: the results I am going to describe are not yet published and so have not yet been subject to peer scrutiny.

Sure enough, we found that in failing states projects were much less likely to succeed. But our question was whether anything could be done about it—anything, that is, that was within the donor's ability to control. It could, for example, be the type of project, or it could be how the project was implemented. It turned out that money spent by the agencies on project supervision has been differentially effective in failing states. It is this differential effectiveness that is the key result. If you put together the much lower success rate of projects in failing states with the differential effectiveness of supervision, then there is a clear implication for how an aid agency should function. Supervision costs money: it comes from the administrative budgets of aid agencies. So an implication is that when agencies operate in failing states, they should budget for a considerably higher ratio of administrative costs to money actually disbursed. Of course, agencies are under pressure to reduce their administrative costs relative to the money they disburse; this is sometimes used as a measure of agency efficiency. But it is misplaced. The environments in which agencies should increasingly be operating are those in which to be effective they will need to spend more on administration, not less. Mismeasurement of bureaucratic performance is a general problem. In aid agencies it encourages low-risk, low-administration operations that are the precise opposite of what they will need to be doing to meet the coming development challenges.

There is one other approach I would like to see tried in failing states, and that is what is known as "independent service authorities." The idea is that in countries where basic public services such as primary education and health clinics are utterly failing, the government, civil society, and donors combined could try to build an alternative system for spending public money. The key features would be a high degree of scrutiny by civil society as to how the money was being spent; competing channels of service delivery, encompassing public, private, and NGO; and continuous evaluation to see which was working best. The authority would be a wholesale organization for purchasing basic services, buying some from local governments, some from NGOs such as churches, and some from private firms. It would finance not just the building of schools and clinics but also their day-to-day operation. Once such an organization was put into place, managed jointly by government, donors, and civil society, both donors and the government would channel money through it. As it demonstrated that it was spending money well, donors would increase the flow of money. If performance deteriorated, the donor money would dry up. Not all governments of failing states would be willing to go along with such a model, but some would. It has not been tried yet, but let me give you an example that briefly got halfway there. The Chad-Cameroon oil pipeline has become a cause célèbre because the NGOs, quite rightly, worried that oil money going to the government of Chad would not be well spent. Indeed, it was more likely to deepen problems than resolve them. The attempted solution was the creation of a system of civil society scrutiny, known as the Collège de Contrôle et de Surveillance des Ressources Pétrolières. The oil money flowed into an account controlled by the Collège, which had to approve all expenditures. The expenditures were restricted by law to social priorities such as health and education. The evidence that this system was basically effective is that within months of it coming into operation in January 2005 the government of Chad changed it. Unsurprisingly, it wanted to make "security" a priority—read money for the military. The Collège was evidently effectively restraining the government from spending the oil money on the military; otherwise why go through the embarrassment and penalties involved in changing the law? Thus we can think of the Collège for the Chad-Cameroon pipeline as a proto–independent service authority. Paradoxically, although the idea has been tried only for oil revenue, it is much better suited for aid. The reason harks back to the time consistency problem that we have already encountered in other contexts. The

Chad deal was unfortunately not time consistent. The deal was that the government of Chad would pass a law establishing the Collège, and in return the oil companies would sink $4.2 billion of investment into oil extraction. Now ask yourself which of these is easier to reverse, the law or the investment. Once you have answered that, you have understood the time consistency problem and can see why it would not be such a problem if instead of oil it was aid. With aid you do not have to sink $4.2 billion in order to get started. It is just a flow of money that can be switched off, unlike the flow of oil. Knowing this, the government has no incentive to tear up the deal. What is the downside of an independent service authority? Well, it is that you start afresh rather than trying to reform the government ministries step by step from within the system, and so it is appropriate only when things are really bad and unlikely to get better by incremental means. So, to be clear, I do not want these authorities everywhere in the bottom billion. I want them to be an option in the worst settings, where the realistic prospect is that otherwise we are going to wait a long time for significant change. I call them independent service authorities for a reason—many governments have already established agencies called independent *revenue* authorities whose function is to raise tax revenue. The function was taken out of the traditional civil service for precisely the reason that I want basic public services to be taken out of the traditional civil service—there was no realistic prospect of the traditional system being made to work. Why did governments go for the radical option on revenue but not on service delivery? The answer is depressingly obvious: governments benefit from the revenue, whereas ordinary people benefit from basic services. Governments were not prepared to let the traditional civil service continue to sabotage tax revenues, because governments themselves were the victims. They *were* prepared to leave basic service delivery unreformed because the governing elite got its services elsewhere.

Aid and Marginalization

In Chapter 6 I argued that globalization was actually making things harder for the bottom billion. Export diversification has become more difficult because of China and India. Capital flight has become easier because of global financial integration. Emigration has become more attractive as the rich-poor gap has widened and more feasible as diasporas from the bottom billion have become established in the West. Hence, even countries that escaped from the traps might find themselves in limbo, unable to replicate the success of poor countries twenty years ago. How does aid affect this marginalization?

The major concern about aid is that it exacerbates the problem of breaking into global markets for new exports. This is due to Dutch disease, which I discussed back in Chapter 3. Aid, like natural resource revenues, tends to make other exports uncompetitive. The IMF feels so strongly about this that its current chief economist, Raghuram Rajan, a smart academic on leave from the University of Chicago's business school, launched a blistering public critique of aid in June 2005, just ahead of the G8 summit. It became a front-page headline in the *Financial Times*. His research showed that aid tended to retard the growth of labor-intensive export activities, precisely the activities needed for diversification in the bottom billion. So there is indeed a problem, and it has to be faced rather than denied. Fortunately, quite a lot can be done about it.

For a start, the aid can be spent on helping the export sector—for example, improving infrastructure at the ports. Even if such aid causes Dutch disease while it is being spent, once the port is improved and the aid is scaled back, there is no further Dutch disease, just a better port. What is required is a once-and-for-all big push, country by country. Such aid would be targeted at lowering the costs that potential exporters would face. It does not make sense to attempt such an approach everywhere. The landlocked and the resource-rich are likely to be out of the game, and there is little point in spending aid to try to get them into it. And even among the coastal, resource-scarce countries, those with really bad governance and policies may be out of it (although the experience of Bangladesh, previously described, suggests that poor governance is not necessarily a killer for exporting). The bottom billion would look a lot more hopeful if a few of their coastal economies really started to take off in global markets. Pioneering success is a sensible use of aid money partly because of the demonstration effect of role models. And remember, unless the coastal countries do well, the landlocked have few options. A big aid push for exporting is a risky venture, because until it is tried there is simply no way of knowing whether it would work. In my view it is well worth the risk, but like other risky uses of aid, it simply will not happen under present incentives for aid agencies. Concentrating aid for a few years in a few countries and spending it on a strategy for export growth just breaks too many of the rules—not only the rules of caution that I have already discussed but also the rules of fair shares. Agencies operate with two types of fair-shares rules. One is for countries: it is difficult to privilege one country over another, even temporarily, although if the Krugman-Venables thesis of agglomeration economies is right, then one of its implications is that such temporary concentrations of aid are likely to be efficient. The other type of fair-shares rule may be even more difficult to surmount: fair shares among internal agency interests. Every aid agency is divided into fiefdoms—rural development, education, health, and so forth. Trying to get an aid agency to focus its resources on an export growth strategy runs afoul of all these interests, for if there is more money to be spent on the country, you can be absolutely sure that the rural development group will lobby for its share of the spending, whether that is important for export growth or not, and the same is true of the education group, the health group, and all the others. In bureaucracies, spending means jobs, promotions, success; it is how, in practice, staff measure themselves. So the present aid system is designed for incrementalism—a bit more budget here, a bit more budget there—and not for structural change. Yet we know that incrementalism is doomed because of diminishing returns to aid. Just doing more of the same is likely to yield a pretty modest payoff. For aid to promote structural change in countries requires structural change in aid agencies.

What else can be done to offset Dutch disease? Well, the aid can be spent on activities that have a large import content. Aid automatically increases the supply of imports, but depending on what you use it for, it can also increase the demand for imports. That is one advantage of technical assistance: it is all directly spent on the import of skills and so does not cause any Dutch disease. Aid spent on infrastructure will have a much higher import content than aid spent on education and so will cause less Dutch disease, dollar for dollar.

Finally, the adverse effects of aid can to an extent be offset by changes in trade policy, but I will come to that in Chapter 10.

Is Aid Part of the Problem or Part of the Solution?

One of the bugbears of the political right is that aid is going into Swiss bank accounts. Sometimes it does; there are well-documented cases. But what is the general relationship? Is aid financing capital flight, as it is financing military spending? Again, in the end it is an empirical question, not something that you can deduce from the first principles of an ideology. It's easy to think of ways in which aid might leak out into capital flight; for example, the president just steals it. But there are also ways in which aid could reduce capital flight. It is true that for this you have to think a little bit harder, as the image of the president stuffing dollars into his briefcase comes more easily, but here is an alternative mechanism. Aid improves the opportunities for private investment, and so money that otherwise would have fled the country gets invested inside it. That is evidently quite possible. The question is which predominates empirically.

For this project I teamed up again with Anke and Cathy. We had all worked on capital flight together twice before, and by now we knew how to control for two-way causation in interpreting the effects of aid. (I should note that at this stage, we have had our work reviewed by anonymous referees for a professional journal and the comments have been sufficiently encouraging for us to continue the process of revision, but it has not yet been published.) Our results indicate that aid significantly *reduced* capital flight. This surprised us, probably because that powerful image of the president stuffing his briefcase had penetrated our minds too. In fact, it seems that aid makes private investment more attractive and so helps to keep capital in the country. Aid, however, is not the only answer to the problems of the bottom billion. In recent years it has probably been overemphasized, partly because it is the easiest thing for the Western world to do and partly because it fits so comfortably into a moral universe organized around the principles of sin and expiation. That overemphasis, which comes from the left, has produced a predictable backlash from the right. Aid does have serious problems, and more especially serious limitations. Alone it will not be sufficient to turn the societies of the bottom billion around. But it is part of the solution rather than part of the problem. The challenge is to complement it with other actions.

CHAPTER **8**

Military Intervention

AFTER IRAQ IT IS DIFFICULT to arouse much support for military intervention. For me this chapter is the toughest in the book because I want to persuade you that external military intervention has an important place in helping the societies of the bottom billion, and that these countries' own military forces are more often part of the problem than a substitute for external forces.

What External Forces Can Do

Until around 1990 international military intervention into failing states was just an extension of the Cold War. The Soviet Union armed the government of Angola, via Cuba, and the United States armed the Angolan rebel group UNITA, via South Africa. These interventions certainly did not help Angola. Only after the end of the Cold War did it become possible for military intervention to be motivated by different considerations. The 1990s began well for military intervention—the expulsion of the Iraqi invasion of Kuwait was a triumph of the new internationalism. Kuwait was a pretty clear-cut case for international intervention: expelling an aggressor. But there are three other important roles for external military intervention: restoration of order, maintaining postconflict peace, and preventing coups.

The Restoration of Order

After Kuwait came another situation that I regard as a clear-cut case for intervention: the restoration of order in a collapsed state. Total collapses are rare, but they happen. In this case it was Somalia. I say the case for this was clear-cut because it is surely irresponsible to leave a huge territory such as Somalia with no government. So did the United States, which sent in its forces under Operation Restore Hope.

Perhaps the U.S. military was overconfident after the huge success in Kuwait, or perhaps it got overruled by the politicians. In any case, the media-intensive military intervention—the invasion of Somalia by U.S. forces was actually delayed by twenty-four hours so that film crews could get ashore in Somalia ahead of the troops—surely invited hubris. Perhaps the scale of intervention was inadequate for the security problems it encountered, but given the media coverage, the eighteen U.S. fatalities that were repeatedly displayed on television doomed the intervention. Don't get me wrong: it is terrible when peacekeeping troops get killed, and it is magnificent of a nation to send its troops into a dangerous situation. But that is what modern armies are for: to supply the global public good of peace in territories that otherwise have the potential for nightmare. Sometimes soldiers will die in the line of duty, and those who do are heroes to be honored, but armies cannot function productively at zero risk. Anyway, what had perhaps been planned as a great media coup for the U.S. presidency had by October 1993 become a media nightmare, and U.S. forces were promptly pulled out. Of course, post-Iraq, the fact that the United States pulled out of Somalia as a result of a mere eighteen deaths looks even more bizarre, but that is what happened.

The consequences for Somalia were miserable: more than twelve years later it still has no functioning national government. By 1995 around 300,000 people had died, and beyond that there are no estimates of the deaths from continuing conflict and the failure of health systems. But the biggest killer consequence upon the withdrawal was not what happened in Somalia but the lesson that was learned: never intervene.

It took only months to prove how disastrously wrong this lesson was. Remember that 1994 was the year of Rwanda. We didn't want a second

Somalia, with another eighteen American soldiers killed, so we got Rwanda, in which half a million people were butchered, entirely avoidably, because international intervention was inadequate. This chapter is written for people who cannot imagine that it is better for half a million Rwandans to have died than for eighteen Americans to be sacrificed. But there is another factor to consider, too: the consequences of civil war spill over to the rich world in the form of epidemics, terrorism, and drugs. Some citizens of the rich world are going to die as a result of chaos in the bottom billion. The choice is whether these deaths will be among civilians as victims of the spillovers or among soldiers who have volunteered to put things right. And there have been spillovers from Somalia. As a result of the continuing chaos, there has been an exodus of young Somali men to developed countries. In July 2005 one of them, an asylum seeker in Britain, filled his rucksack with explosives and tried to blow up commuters on the London Underground. In November 2005 a Somali gang murdered a policewoman in a bank robbery in Bradford, United Kingdom. I have a young son, and when he is older I don't want him to be exposed to the risks of being a peacekeeping soldier. But I don't want him exposed to the risk of being blown apart in London or shot in Bradford by some exile from a failing state, either. Nor do I want him exposed to the risk of disease. Somalia was the last place on earth to be home to smallpox. It was eliminated there by international health interventions a few years before the Somali state collapsed. Now such elimination would not be possible. Had the Somali state not lasted as long as it did, we would still have smallpox. On balance, I think that my child, and everyone else's, will be safer if we respond to the problem of failing states by restoring order, rather than by relying only on the myriad of defensive measures that we need if we don't.

Maintaining Postconflict Peace

After Rwanda, military intervention was back in business, and the new role was the maintenance of peace after conflict ended. It was pretty hit-and-miss: some places got lots of troops, others not many. About the highest ratio in the world of foreign peacekeepers to population was in East Timor. One peacekeeper I met there was from Gambia, one of the smallest and poorest countries in Africa. When I asked him about the situation in East Timor, he told me that it was terrible. "These people are *really* poor," he said. If he thought so, they were. Later, when I met up with the diplomatic set, I asked why there were so many peacekeepers in that country. The answer I got about summed up the problems of foreign military intervention: because it was safe there. Governments that send soldiers to serve as UN peacekeepers are paid $1,000 per individual per month. For some countries this is not a bad way of getting some income from their armies. The imperative is then that soldiers should not get themselves killed, so safe environments such as East Timor are ideal, and risky environments such as the Democratic Republic of the Congo are unattractive. Even if troops are sent to dangerous places, they often play it safe. The best-known example occurred near Srebrenica in Bosnia in 1995, where Dutch troops were supposed to be providing a safe haven but failed to protect the scared refugees, who were massacred. The Dutch seem not to have learned a lesson from this—when Liberia looked worrying in 2004, as it has periodically in recent years, the Dutch sent a naval vessel, but their instructions were, broadly, to sail away if trouble developed. Another revealing case is the ragtag United Nations force in Sierra Leone. In 2000 the RUF rebel movement took five hundred of these soldiers hostage and stripped them of their military equipment. Was the RUF such a formidable fighting force? Hardly—once a few hundred British troops arrived a few months later, willing to take casualties, the whole rebel army rapidly collapsed. The UN troops were an easy target because the RUF understood that they would not resist. They were carrying their guns like tourists flaunting their jewelry.

So much for how not to provide international military intervention. By contrast, the British intervention in Sierra Leone just mentioned, Operation Palliser, has been a huge success. It has imposed security and maintained it once the RUF was disposed of. The whole operation has been amazingly cheap. I can think of no other way in which peace could have been restored and maintained in Sierra Leone. Anke Hoeffler and I even tried to do a cost-benefit analysis of the operation. Finding out about the costs was surprisingly easy—I simply phoned the Foreign Office, and not only did they more or less know, they more or less told me. The harder part was to estimate the benefits. After all, nothing much had happened in

Sierra Leone since the British troops established peace. This, of course, was the point. Without them there would have been some probability that plenty of very bad things would have happened. That avoided probability is the key to the payoff to British troops. We used our model of conflict to estimate the likely risk of reversion to conflict in Sierra Leone—admittedly a pretty crude approximation because we used the model of a typical postconflict country, which ignores the particularities of Sierra Leone. But as a way of estimating a representative payoff to postconflict interventions, sidestepping the particularities is not such a bad thing. We then took this avoided probability of conflict and multiplied it by the typical cost of a civil war, already estimated at around $64 billion. I have to say that I do not like making calculations such as this; our model is better used to establish which policy interventions might typically work than to estimate risks in any particular case, because there is so much important information about each situation that a model must omit. But for what it's worth, we estimated that the benefits of intervention were around thirty times its cost. With a cost-benefit ratio like that, there is quite a bit of room for error in the calculations before they become misleading.

Operation Palliser was brilliant, and the British army can be proud of its contribution to the development of Sierra Leone. It also serves as a model for military intervention in the bottom billion: cheap, confident, and sustained. It was welcome, too—the people of the country were truly thankful. Yet it is completely uncelebrated. Instead, reverberating in the newspaper headlines each day is Iraq. As with Somalia, the apparent lesson from Iraq is to never intervene. That is not just the popular reaction but also the reaction of the insiders. In November 2005 I was invited to Brussels to address a bunch of specialists, and the room was awash with military braid. When I made my pitch on Sierra Leone, the first response was, "But surely that's been blown out of the water by Iraq." The important thing to remember, though, is that we've already discovered what happens when we stick our heads as deep in the sand as they will go: we get Rwanda.

So we should intervene, but not necessarily everywhere. Sierra Leone rather than Iraq is the likely future of intervention opportunities in the bottom-billion countries. Look at the contrasts between the two situations. In Sierra Leone our forces were invited in by the government and hugely welcomed by the local population. In Sierra Leone we could not be accused of going in for the oil, as there wasn't any. In Sierra Leone we did not have to worry about "fixing what we broke," for there was not much to break, and we ousted the RUF with minimal damage. In Sierra Leone we needed less than a thousand proper soldiers to achieve decisive military change. The differences seem obvious.

Protection Against Coups

It is politically correct to argue that the military forces of the rich countries no longer have a role in the bottom-billion countries. Indeed, for fear of arousing anticolonialist sentiments the French have got themselves into the odd position of maintaining large military forces in Africa that they dare not use. For example, in 1999 they let the head of the tiny army in Côte d'Ivoire, Robert Gueï, mount a successful coup against the legitimate government despite having two thousand troops stationed in the country. To keep the French forces in their barracks, the coup leader promised to hold an election within six months. And so the French decided to let the coup succeed—after all, it was only for a little while. Evidently, the French government was not aware of the problem of time inconsistency: that sometimes the incentive to break a promise is overwhelming. To be fair, the coup leader did stick to the letter of his promise and held an election. But he put himself forward as a candidate and banned both of the country's most prominent political leaders from running. As you might imagine, this did not produce a happy outcome, and so the French army did eventually have to intervene to prevent a rebel group from seizing the capital. But instead of either putting down the rebellion or forcing a compromise settlement, the French simply held a line separating the government and rebel forces, yielding a de facto partition of the country that has now persisted for several years. Each side has used the respite to rearm; after doing so, the government attacked the French forces, since they saw them as protecting the rebels.

The French hesitation to intervene is mirrored in the deployment of the European Union's new rapid reaction force. Ostensibly this force is for deployment in African emergencies. I suspect that it will never be deployed. For example, it has not been used in Darfur, Sudan, where government-backed militias are currently slaughtering and terrorizing the region's people, nor to put down the August 2005 coup in Mauritania. Its creation allows Europe to present the impression that it is doing something, just as the continuing French military presence in Africa creates the illusion of French power. But in reality these forces are impotent because Europe does not have an authorizing environment for their use. The United Nations does, but actually for many bottom-billion environments we can do better: we could turn to the regional political groupings. Most of the costs of state failure accrue to neighbors—that is, state failure is a regional public bad. So it is the region that has the strongest interest to do something about it. But in Africa no country really has the resources or the political ascendancy to impose order on failing neighbors. So the European Union has the forces and the aspirations, and the affected regions have the interests and can confer legitimacy. This situation has the potential for a marriage: the African Union could provide the political authority for military intervention, and the European rapid reaction force could be the backbone of whatever force was used to intervene. I will give an example of what I have in mind, something that almost worked out well, but didn't: Togo.

Togo was ruled as the personal fiefdom of a dictator, Gnassingbé Eyadéma, for thirty-eight years, a longer continuous period of rule than anywhere else other than Cuba. His rule was economically ruinous as well as politically stifling. He died in February 2005, and his son, Faure Gnassingbé, declared himself president. At this point the African Union, to its considerable credit, classified the event as a coup and insisted on a constitutional process. The African Union had sufficient power relative to Togo that Gnassingbé agreed to elections. Triumph? Nearly. Gnassingbé decided not only that he would be a candidate in the elections but that he would run them. To nobody's great surprise he announced himself the winner, though had he actually taken the trouble to count the votes he would have discovered that he had lost. So what should have happened? Well, surely what should have happened is that once the African Union had declared the coup unconstitutional, an international military force should have arrived promptly in the country to take temporary power. It really would not have needed to be a very big force. Speed would have been more important than size. In fact, what was needed was a rapid reaction force, which the European Union already had. A temporary military intervention would have supervised free and fair elections. Nobody could have accused such an intervention of being neocolonialist, as the international force would not have been trying to colonize Togo. It would have sat there for perhaps four months. As it is, the world may have to wait a good long time until Gnassingbé makes his own decisive contribution to its development by dying, for he was thirty-eight when he became president.

Coups such as the one that destabilized Côte d'Ivoire are still a problem for the bottom billion. Remember, they are driven by much the same factors as rebellions are: poverty and stagnation. And yet it would be relatively easy to make coups history. We just need a credible military guarantee of external intervention. Obviously the European Union is not going to offer a blank check to every regime in the bottom billion. But we could offer a guarantee to democratic governments conditional upon internationally certified free and fair elections. I will spell out the conditions we might specify in Chapter 10, on international norms.

Are Domestic Militaries a Substitute?

You might well be prepared to accept that in extreme situations such as Somalia, where there is a total breakdown of authority, there is a need for external intervention. But as for postconflict situations and the risk of coups, why don't the governments of the bottom billion rely upon their own security forces? Well, because in precisely the situations where governments face the greatest risks their own military establishments are not the solution but rather part of the problem.

Peace Through Strength?

Back in Chapter 2 I discussed the risk that postconflict situations might revert to conflict. It's a substantial risk, and postconflict governments know it. Typically what they do is to keep their military spending high—almost as high as during the war itself. They forgo the chance of a peace dividend, thinking it too risky. This is a natural reaction, and you can see it on the ground—high levels of domestic military spending are typical in postconflict situations. But this could just be inertia. I wondered whether it would be possible to test whether governments set their levels of military spending specifically in response to the risk of civil war. Anke and I were already working in the specialized world of military spending in order to determine whether it was financed by aid, as I discussed in Chapter 7. And we had already modeled the risk of civil war, as you saw in Chapter 2. We now brought the two together. Sure enough, the level of military spending that a government chose reflected the risk of civil war that it faced. Postconflict governments were spending more on the military largely because they faced abnormally high risks. Then we decided to confront the issue of whether this high level of postconflict military spending was effective in deterring conflict. This was not an easy question to answer because obviously the governments that spend the most are likely to be those that face the biggest risks. As a result, unless military spending is totally effective, high spending will be correlated with reversion to conflict. In other words, because causality runs from risk to spending, it is hard to distinguish any causality from spending to risk. We think we managed to overcome this problem, and our published results indicate that high military spending in postconflict situations is part of the problem, not part of the solution. It makes further conflict substantially more likely. It is natural for a postconflict government to try to defend itself, but it doesn't work. We have an idea of what goes wrong, and it involves time inconsistency. In postconflict situations neither side trusts the other. The rebels face the greater problem because governments can maintain their armies during peace much more easily than can the rebels. So although the government has an incentive to promise an inclusive peace deal, as time goes on it has less and less of an incentive to keep its word. As a result, there are sure to be factions among the rebel forces wanting to go back to war preemptively, while the option is still open. High military spending by the government may inadvertently signal to the rebel forces that the government is indeed going to renege on any deal and rule by repression.

I was once brought in to talk to a depressingly large group of finance ministers from postconflict countries, and I put to them this argument that high military spending is likely to be dysfunctional. Despite the fact that military spending is often a taboo subject, there was an enthusiastic chorus of approval led by the finance minister of Mozambique, Luisa Diogo. Now prime minister, Diogo gave us the example of her own country. Completely bucking the usual trend, her government had radically cut military spending to virtually nothing, and the peace had endured. It turned out that, far from favoring big military budgets, finance ministers wanted evidence to defend their spending priorities against the demands of the powerful military lobby.

The key implication is that in postconflict situations risks are high. Governments recognize these risks. Eventually, if they run the economy well, this will bring the risk down, but it is going to take around a decade. There is no magic political fix, and so there has to be some military force to keep the peace during this dangerous period. But if the force is domestic, it exacerbates the problem. In the typical postconflict situation external military force is needed for a long time.

Grand Extortion

One obvious feature of coups is that they are perpetrated by the military. Our work on coups and on military spending shows pretty straightforwardly that after a successful coup the new leaders slam up military spending. But Anke and I wondered whether in response to a high risk of a coup governments tried to buy the military off. If this was the case, the military would, in effect, be running a protection racket on a grand scale. We termed this grand extortion. So we had a clear question: did a high risk of a coup drive up military budgets? Again, it was not an easy question to answer. Our research (which is still new and as yet unpublished) revealed that behavior was distinctive in the governments of the bottom billion. In countries that are richer than the bottom billion the risk of a coup is small, and if it increases a little, the military budget is not increased—indeed, if anything the military gets cut if it starts to be a nuisance. By contrast, in the countries of the bottom billion coup risk is generally much higher. The threat from the military is indeed probably the biggest risk of losing power that most of these governments face. And they pay up: more risk induces more money for the military.

If, however, we are right, then governments in the bottom billion are in a bind. They are genuinely threatened by their own armies, and so, threatened by grand extortion, they pay up. I say "they" pay up, but remember from Chapter 7 than in many of the bottom-billion countries around 40 percent of military spending is inadvertently financed by aid. So actually, we in the West pay up. The militaries of the bottom billion are running an extortion racket and our aid programs are the victim. Coups are usually a dysfunctional way of changing government, and that is the core reason why we need to provide external military guarantees against them. But we might also bear in mind that if we provided military guarantees, the protection rackets would collapse. Governments could spend our aid on development instead of extortion.

CHAPTER 9

Laws and Charters

SO FAR I HAVE LOOKED at aid and at military interventions. Both are useful, but both are pretty costly, one in money and the other in guts: political guts, and sometimes soldiers' guts. Now I am going to look at a range of interventions that are strikingly cheap. They fall into two groups: changes in our own laws that would benefit the bottom billion, and the generation of international norms that would help to guide behavior.

Our Laws, Their Problems

In Chapter 1 I discussed the danger that the societies of the bottom billion might become safe havens for criminals, terrorists, and disease. Paradoxically, some of this is reciprocal: the rich countries have been a safe haven for the criminals of the bottom billion.

One grotesque form of this safe haven role has been that Western banks have taken deposits looted from the bottom-billion societies, held the money in great secrecy, and refused to give it back. Many Western countries are incriminated in this shameful practice. In the United States it came to light in 2004 that Riggs Bank, in Washington, D.C., was holding huge deposits from the president of Equatorial Guinea and writing him cringingly effusive letters of encouragement. As soon as the matter came to light it was stopped and the bank radically reorganized. In Britain, it was revealed in 2000 that the family of Sani Abacha, a former military dictator of

Nigeria, had made massive cash deposits into London banks with no troubling questions whatsoever. But probably the all-time prize goes to Switzerland. Also around 2000, it came out that Abacha had placed money there as well before his death in 1998. When the post-Abacha Nigerian government pursued the money, the Swiss did not exactly cooperate. Even after a Swiss court eventually ruled that the deposits belonged to the government of Nigeria, the Swiss minister of justice refused to return the money. He had to be shamed into doing so. Does Switzerland really need to make a living this way?

The costs and complexities of getting corrupt money repatriated make the process prohibitive in all but the most dramatic and publicized cases. Is changing this at all feasible? If we made the reporting of any potentially corrupt deposits a requirement of banking, and if we made the freezing and repatriation of those deposits radically easier, would it seriously damage our financial system? I doubt it, because if the money is suspected of having a connection to terrorism we already do it. The West's current concern is terrorism, so we do something about it. The problem of governance in the bottom billion is not seen as ours, and so we do the minimum. Consequently, corrupt politicians in the bottom billion continue to stack their money away in Western banks. Of course, most bankers are people of integrity. But the banking profession has a responsibility to clean up its act, just as De Beers did in respect to diamonds. At present, a small minority of bankers are living on the profits from holding deposits of corrupt money. We have a word for people who live on the immoral earnings of others: pimps. Pimping bankers are no better than any other sort of pimp. They have to be driven out of banking, and it is primarily the responsibility of the banking profession itself to do it, for it's the bankers who have the inside knowledge, just as the main defense against quacks is the medical profession. The agency with official responsibility for oversight of the financial sector is usually the central bank. Central banks are about as far removed from aid agencies as it is possible to get while still being agencies within the same government. For example, politically, the staffs of aid agencies are on the far left of government, while central bankers are on the far right. Aid agencies have little choice but to focus on the bottom billion; they are not going to be able to duck the problem. But central bankers will most surely be able to duck it, claiming it has nothing to do with them and that their priorities lie elsewhere. Somehow, the central banks have to get this onto their agenda.

It is not just the banks. Until very recently, if a French company bribed a public official in a bottom-billion society, the payment was tax deductible. Think it through: French taxpayers were subsidizing bribery. Of course, it did not apply to the same behavior within France: if a French company had reported that it had bribed a French politician, the consequence would have been a criminal investigation, not a reduced tax bill. France was not alone in this practice. No Western government wanted to force its companies to behave properly because there was the reasonable fear that this would disadvantage its companies in winning contracts. The great commercial game in bottom-billion societies has been to bribe your way into a lucrative contract. This is an instance of a coordination problem that game theorists call the prisoner's dilemma. We would all be better off in a world in which our companies did not bribe the governments of the bottom billion, but the worst outcome is for the companies in one nation to refrain from bribing while those of other nations continue. And so for a long time we were all locked into bribery.

Eventually, after a lot of pressure, in 1999 the OECD managed to organize the necessary coordination to escape this dilemma: an agreement among its member governments that they would all legislate to make bribery of a public official in a foreign country an offense. The question is now how vigorously this legislation will be enforced. Again, all the incentives at the corporate and country level are not to cause trouble. At least bribes are no longer tax deductible. But of course it is very easy to dress up a bribe as a "facilitation payment" for some service. It is only when whistleblowers within a company have an incentive to report the truth that the law can be properly enforced. Within government, this sort of work comes under the responsibility of the department that deals with trade and industry. These departments see their external role as helping to win exports. It is hard to get them to worry about the impact of their actions on the governance of the bottom billion. Like central banks, they do not see it as their problem.

Corruption has its epicenters. I started by focusing on our banks, where much of the loot is deposited. Among the companies that pay the bribes two sectors seem to stand out: resource extraction and construction. I will discuss how to deal with the problems of resource extraction shortly; it has been publicly recognized as a problem at least since the launch of the Extractive Industries Transparency Initiative by Britain's Tony Blair in 2002. By contrast, corruption in the construction sector has been a dirty secret. Transparency International decided to bring it to greater prominence by devoting its *Global Corruption Report 2005* to the sector. Construction has all the ingredients conducive to corruption: each project is a one-time-only thing, and so cannot readily be priced. There are so many uncertainties in execution that it is not possible to draw up what economists refer to as a "complete contract." As a result, it is easy to evade the discipline that would otherwise be imposed by competitive tendering. A crooked construction company colludes with a public official to win the contract with an artificially low bid, but then they recontract on points of detail that crop up during construction. A friend of mine was finance minister in Eritrea, at the time one of the least corrupt of the bottom-billion countries. Even so, he realized that he would not be able to prevent corruption in construction projects, and that this would undermine governance more widely. His drastic solution was to minimize spending on construction, vetoing projects wherever possible. He was not foolish. There are now credible studies for some countries that estimate how much corruption in the construction sector is raising the cost of infrastructure and thereby reducing growth, and these effects are large.

Why is corruption in the construction sector particularly important now for the bottom billion? Well, the Gleneagles G8 summit in July 2005 announced a doubling of aid, focused on infrastructure. As this gets implemented there is going to be a massive construction boom in many of these countries. Under present circumstances, this will amplify what is already a serious problem of misgovernance. Corrupt money is not just a waste. Think back to the natural resource trap. Big corrupt money is likely to undermine the political process, enabling the strategy of patronage to triumph over honest politics. Aid for infrastructure makes sense, but only if it is matched by a radical tightening of the enforcement of anticorruption norms and regulations in the construction sector. The construction companies are largely our companies. Their behavior depends upon our laws and how they are enforced.

Norms for the Bottom Billion: Making International Standards and Codes Pertinent

Most conduct is guided by norms rather than by laws. Norms are voluntary and are effective because they are enforced by peer pressure. Over the past fifty years the world has generated a huge range of them, enshrined in international standards and codes. Most of these are voluntary; others ultimately have the force of law and so curtail national sovereignty but are largely enforced by peer pressure rather than by legal penalties. Norms can be massively effective in inducing changes in governance. To see how effective, look at Eastern Europe over the past decade. The typical situation was that the countries of Eastern Europe, having escaped from the Soviet bloc, wanted to lock themselves into being market democracies. They had one hugely attractive option to hand: membership in the European Union (called the European Community until 1992). But the EU had an established set of rules, the *acquis communautaires,* to which all new members had to adhere. Over the course of a decade, the countries of Eastern Europe made a massive effort to change their societies into market democracies in order to meet these standards and so have a chance of becoming members. This was the power of a set of international norms at its most stunning. If you want to understand why some countries of the former Soviet Union have done well while others are becoming failing states, a pretty good guide is geography. The further away from the EU and so the less credible the prospect of EU membership, the worse they have done. The societies of the bottom billion need some set of norms that are analogous to the EU effect.

They do not, however, literally need the *acquis communautaires.* These rules were written for western Europe. The countries of the bottom billion need rules that are appropriate for societies at their level of development, that address the problems they face. There are lots of standards and codes, but mostly they codify desirable behavior for either the already developed countries or the emerging market economies. The societies of the bottom billion have different problems and need different norms. In this chapter I am going to focus on what norms really matter for them. How to get these norms adopted is going to be deferred until Part 5. I am going to propose five international charters—norms that I think would help reformers within the societies of the bottom billion to achieve and sustain change.

A Charter for Natural Resource Revenues

In Chapter 3, I set out what goes wrong in resource-rich countries. International standards are our best hope of helping reformers within these societies to put things right, and the payoff would be huge. Resource revenues to the bottom billion are bigger than aid, and far more poorly used. If we could raise the effectiveness of resource revenues even to the present level of aid effectiveness, the impact would be enormous. The British government has already made a start on proposing international standards, launching the Extractive Industries Transparency Initiative in 2002. This is a good start, but only a start. What should a more comprehensive charter say?

Let's explore the chain from undiscovered resources in the ground to the basic public services that they could finance. Step one is awarding the contracts to get the resources out of the ground. This step has usually been a disaster: companies have bribed their way into contracts that are lucrative for them and for the bribed politicians but lousy for the country. Tufts University economist Maggie McMillan has managed, thanks to the much greater freedom of information in the United States than elsewhere, to get data on the international investment returns of U.S. oil companies. She is finding that their returns have been higher the worse the governance of the countries in which they operate. Of course, the companies will explain this as compensation for risk, and in part it is. But it also probably reflects the returns to the lack of transparent competition. An oil field in a developed country is auctioned off in a transparent process. This should be a basic requirement of an international charter on resource extraction. Since the design of auctions is complicated and apparently transparent processes can still be corrupt, a charter could usefully spell out some of the key features of an effective process.

Step two is what the contracts say—in particular, who bears what risk. At present, price risk is borne by governments, not by companies. Tiny countries, with governments that lack the competence to manage even a village post office, are trying to cope with boom-bust cycles, rather than the task being done by the financially sophisticated and huge oil companies at the other end of the contract. It does not have to be like that. Oil companies could bear at least part of the price risk—for example, undertaking to provide a set quantity of oil at the world price averaged over several years, thereby stabilizing a component of total oil revenue.

Step three is to make all payments of revenue transparent. This has been the focus of the Extractive Industries Transparency Initiative and of its precursor, the Publish What You Pay campaign. It was the right place to start. Unless citizens know what money is coming in, they have little hope of scrutinizing how it is used. All companies must be included, most especially the national oil companies that are sometimes governments within governments. There is also a need for some honest broker to collate the individual company information into a coherent picture of flows into government. For example, in Angola there are thirty-four foreign oil companies and a state-owned national oil company. It is a skilled job to make sense of the information supplied by each individual company. The obvious agency to do this would be the World Bank or the IMF, as either of these has the expertise and does not stand to gain from falsification. The broker would act merely as an accountant, not as a police officer, converting a confusing morass of information into knowledge that citizens could use.

Step four is transparency in public expenditures. In the resource-rich countries effective public spending is the vital route to development, and this is not going to happen without transparency. Whereas transparency in public spending is always desirable, in the resource-rich countries it is vital. And so there is a need to set out minimum standards of transparency. I spell this out below when I discuss the charter on budgets.

Step five is a set of rules for smoothing public spending in the face of revenue shocks. The history of resource revenue shocks is a pretty sad one: booms have often been the prelude to crises. Astonishingly, given its core role in crisis management and prevention, the IMF has not yet come up with simple guidelines on how to manage volatility in resource revenues. It is true that perfection is elusive and the details can become complex. But a guideline does not have to be so sophisticated in order to be an improvement on what has gone on in the past. At present, resource-rich countries have to come up with their own, ad hoc systems, each different. Often these are the pet project of some reforming minister and do not survive beyond the minister's departure. An international standard would make smoothing arrangements easier to introduce and harder to remove. It is important to distinguish between smoothing out shocks, which is a medium-term strategy, and accumulating financial assets for future generations. Norway, about the richest country in the world, parks some of its oil revenue in a "future-generations fund," and several countries of the bottom billion have sought to imitate it. This may be a good idea for Norway, which has capital coming out of its ears, but it is a pretty doubtful one for the bottom-billion societies, since they are extremely short of capital. They need to learn how to invest their money well domestically, not how to park it in the U.S. stock market. Future-generations funds are even politically risky in low-income countries: as they accumulate they are a mounting temptation for populism. Consequently, future-generations funds are unlikely to make it through to some future generation and more likely to be a transfer from the prudent governments that establish them to the imprudent governments that dismantle them. Sadly, that is what the record to date bears out.

If such a charter were launched, would it have any effect? I first became convinced of the need for a charter when I visited East Timor. The Indonesians had recently pulled out and the new government had yet to be elected. However, the little group of exiles who had returned from Portugal and who formed the provisional government had decided to hold a planning retreat, since East Timor was about to get seriously large oil and gas revenues. The exiles knew that managing the revenues would be difficult, and to their considerable credit they knew that they knew nothing—and had done something about it, looking for a model of how to handle the revenues. If there had been a model spelled out in an international charter, most probably they would have adopted it and turned their attention to some of the other thousand things that a postconflict government has to worry about. But there was no charter. Instead, they used two criteria to find a model, both of which were understandable. The first criterion was that it had to come from a country with oil. It was hard to argue with that one. Criterion number two was that it had to come from a Portuguese-speaking country, so that they could understand it. This also appears to have some logic to it—except that when you put the two criteria together, you come up with Angola. They sent a team to Angola to learn how to manage oil revenues, but they might as well have sent a team to a brothel to learn about sanctity. As it turned out, they had more sense than to use Angola as a model. But unfortunately they used Norway instead. This episode convinced me that a charter would be useful.

And so it has proved. The Extractive Industries Transparency Initiative, which was launched by the British government in 2002 as a proto-charter, has already had an effect. It has been picked up by East Timor and by several West African governments, not least the reform team in Nigeria. I remember attending a meeting of West African ministers at which the governance of oil revenues was discussed. The delegations that were decidedly unenthusiastic about transparency sat there quietly, perhaps hoping to be shielded by an Africa-versus-the-outsiders mentality. It didn't happen. Several of the other African delegations wanted change and committed to transparency. What followed was an intense internal debate within some of the recalcitrant governments on whether or not to commit to the charter. There were evidently some voices within even the worst governments wanting change, just as, unsurprisingly, there were voices wanting the gravy train to continue. Can you imagine that happening without the spur of an international charter? This peer pressure is one way in which international standards might get adopted: as reformers from time to time gain power in bottom-billion countries, they seize their moment to adopt the standards, and then it becomes politically troublesome to abandon them. As more countries adopt them, pressure on the nonadopters grows because they begin to stand out as conniving at corruption.

The main point of pressure for the adoption of international standards would come from within the bottom-billion societies themselves, especially from civil society. An international charter gives people something very concrete to demand: either the government adopts it or it must explain why it won't. All societies of the bottom billion have plenty of latent opposition to bad governance. But transforming this latent opposition into effective pressure is difficult. Even at the best of times such pressure is a public good and so subject to all the problems of free riding—the "why bother, let's leave it to someone else to stick their neck out" attitude. And, of course, in many societies it requires courage as well as effort. What is more, because reform is complicated, people can reasonably disagree on what needs to be done, but such disagreements divide and dissipate the reformist opposition. Often such disagreements elide into disputes over leadership: backing someone else's idea for reform is perceived as acknowledging the other as leader and thus giving up one's own claim. Where villains are in power they should not be underestimated. Not only do they have money, but they are skilled in the tactics of divide and rule. They will be actively trying to create and amplify disagreements. An international standard provides something that all the opposition can coordinate around without conceding leadership to anyone in particular.

A third key pressure point in cleaning up resource revenues is the international companies in the extractive industries. The model here is De Beers and its Kimberley Process for the certification of diamonds. For many years De Beers had been in denial that conflict diamonds were a problem. Then pressure from NGOs persuaded the company that denial was not going to work: if the image of conflict diamonds became entrenched in the mind of consumers, diamonds could go the way of fur. To their considerable credit, De Beers radically changed tack. They came up with a plan for certification, and they are still pressing ahead to make this process more effective. For example, they are promoting a new smart-card technology that can be used to make it far harder for alluvial diamonds, dug up from riverbeds by individual prospectors, to be smuggled. As certification becomes more effective the rents from diamonds can accrue to governments rather than to traders. One expert told me that he thought alluvial miners were currently getting only around 10 percent of the true market price.

De Beers demonstrates that big companies can become a key part of the solution rather than being part of the problem. What worked for diamonds may not work for oil, but in one respect the task of transparency is quite a bit easier: it is far harder to smuggle oil than diamonds. There has been some "conflict oil": at one stage oil worth about a billion dollars a year was being "bunkered"—stolen—from the delta region of Nigeria. But because of the trace elements found in oil, its origin is detectable, and so certification could be effective. Indeed, once the Nigerian government managed to track down where its oil was being sold it was able to curtail the problem.

In another respect, however—the organization of the industry—oil is harder than diamonds. De Beers is far more important to the diamond market than any single oil company is to the oil market. When BP tried to work in a transparent manner in Angola, the Angolan government threatened the other thirty-three oil companies operating there that the first one to follow would be thrown out. None did. Oil companies are too competitive for the industry to organize itself of its own accord. This is where Western civil society comes in. Brent Spar was an oil well in the North Sea that had reached the end of its productive life. Shell, the owner, proposed to discard it in a way that might have damaged the environment. The reaction by European environmentalists was so devastating to Shell's image and sales that it changed its policy on closing oil wells. At first the Shell management tried to stand firm, but then sales of Shell products in Germany crashed by 30 percent, prompting the manager of Shell Germany to break ranks. Where did all this power come from? Well, perhaps it was the accumulated effects of German teenagers in the backseat of the family car, saying, "No, Mom and Dad, not that gas station—did you hear what Shell wants to do?" and the parents presumably thought it was better to avoid the argument. Brent Spar demonstrated that what ordinary people in the West think about oil companies really matters. Those with brand names have spent billions building up their reputation and do not want to see it destroyed. The problem is that at present the pressure is for things that just do not matter very much for the bottom billion. Companies are being pressured on their environmental policies and on their employment policies, both of which are frankly peripheral, when what is needed is pressure on their policies toward governance. If there was an international charter on standards along the lines of the five points laid out above, NGOs could start to demand that companies adhere to it. For example, a company that entered into an extraction contract won without competitive bidding would be censured. Potentially it is even possible for oil companies to be required to display at their gas stations where the oil used in the gasoline is from. Obviously, oil from different sources gets mixed together, but for the purposes of consumer pressure the source of oil is a financial concept, not a physical one. If a thousand barrels of oil from Angola go into a storage tank, one thousand barrels of the oil that comes out could be designated as being from Angola. If consumers refused to buy gasoline "from" Angola, the companies would be reluctant to put it into the storage tanks in the first place. Angolan oil would become harder to sell, except at a discount, and this would create a financial incentive for the Angolan government to be transparent. The same process that so effectively pressured Shell to clean up Brent Spar would be directed to the far more valuable task of making oil revenues effective for development.

Consumer pressure works only on those companies that have brand names to protect. Some don't. I have already raised the specter of the Chinese scrambling for natural resources without much concern for governance. Western consumer pressure is not going to cut much ice with the Chinese, and don't hold your breath waiting for Chinese consumer pressure, either. This is the argument put forth by at least some of the Western oil companies: impose standards on them and all that happens is that the Chinese are let in. Can anything be done about this? I think so. In part what the Chinese government wants is a place at the top table—recognition by the international community that China is a key country, powerful and important. The deal has to be that with power come a few responsibilities, one of which is adherence to international standards for resource extraction. If Western consumers force the big-brand oil companies to adopt international standards, then in turn the oil companies will pressure their governments—the United States, Britain, and France—to come to an arrangement with China. The West has to offer China greater inclusion in power in return for adherence to international standards. It has to be made in China's interests for the bottom billion to develop rather than to fall apart.

A Charter for Democracy

Since the fall of the Soviet Union democracy has spread rapidly across the developing world. Political scientists actually measure it. There is an index called Polity that rates the degree of democracy on a scale from 0 to 10. In the 1980s the average developing county scored only around 2; now the average is around 4.5. However, to date, this transition to democracy has been defined overwhelmingly in terms of elections. This has been inevitable. Electoral competition can be introduced with great speed even in the most unpromising bottom-billion conditions, such as Afghanistan. As the prospect of elections moves toward becoming a reality, many individuals and groups have incentives to behave in ways that facilitate their introduction: they form political parties as a means to acquiring power. But remember, elections are not enough. Electoral competition can make things worse, because patronage will often win out over honest politics in the struggle for votes—recall the survival of the fattest.

By contrast, checks and balances take time to introduce, and they are political orphans: those parties that expect to rule have a direct interest in frustrating their introduction, and the entire political class stands to lose if patronage politics is made infeasible. Elections determine who is in power, but they do not determine how power is used. Because of the different time scales for elections and for checks and balances, the instant democracies must almost inevitably go through a phase in which electoral competition faces few restraints. The real issue is whether this is merely a phase or becomes a permanent feature of the polity—whether these countries get stuck with a parody of democracy.

Why have elections spread around the world? Their spread surely demonstrates the power of international influence, especially that of the international media. Being events, elections get intensively reported. Citizens in the developing world have inevitably come to see an election as the defining feature of democratic legitimacy. Not only does international reporting spread a model that local populations follow, but also it enables them to harness the power of international pressure. Many of the banners at political demonstrations are in English, demonstrating that we are part of the intended audience for these protests. Hence, our message matters, but to date the message has been concerned nearly exclusively with elections. Checks and balances are continuous and complex—they are not events—and so they have been much less newsworthy. The mature democracies now need to use our evident influence to encourage the less visible aspects of democracy.

Since growth itself gradually increases income to the level at which checks and balances are secured, an improvement in them eventually becomes self-sustaining. An international effort to promote checks and balances would therefore only need to be temporary. The wave of electoral competition that swept the developing world in the 1990s, and may now sweep the Middle East, thus needs to be complemented by a wave of enthusiasm for political restraints.

As with resource rents, it would help if there was some international minimum standard, analogous to the minimum standards set out by the European Union. I would start with rules about the media, which are the most effective form of scrutiny. In the societies of the bottom billion the key media are probably the radio channels and increasingly television. One rare and dramatic story from Peru illustrates this. The government of Alberto Fujimori was notably corrupt, so much so that the chief of the secret police, Vladimiro Montesinos, who was charged with the task of implementing all the corruption, decided to keep careful records. These records now provide a very rare quantitative window on political corruption, and John McMillan of Stanford Business School has analyzed them. His work shows that the Fujimori government set out to systematically undermine each check and balance that restrained it. It bribed members of parliament, judges, newspaper editors, and the staff of radio stations and television stations. If there was a restraint, the government undermined it. The amount it was prepared to pay reflected its view of the importance of each restraint. From our perspective it is not just creepily fascinating to see a system of bad governance on display; it also tells us what is really important in the fight against it. Where the Fujimori regime put most of its money is probably where we should be most vigilant. While the official constitutional restraints, such as parliament and the courts, were bought, the regime did not spend serious money undermining them. The newspapers were also bought, but it was the same story: thousands of dollars a month, not millions. Where the zeros rolled out on the checks was to buy the television stations. There were ten stations, and the government bought them at nearly a million dollars each per month. This money bought a proper contract—each day the station had to screen its evening news program in advance for Montesinos and make the required changes. So for the government it was the television news that was the vital restraint to control. Was this paranoia? No, it turned out that the government was quite right. We know because the government had only bothered to buy the nine biggest television channels—it decided not to bother with the tenth, a tiny financial satellite service with only ten thousand subscribers. That is how the government fell. Someone leaked a video of Montesinos bribing a judge, and it was broadcast on this one television channel. Protest escalated uncontrollably. So in Peru the key restraint upon the government was the media, and among the media, it was television. I think that in most bottom-billion countries television is still too limited to be the key medium; it is more likely to be radio. Thus among the checks and balances I would place keeping radio out of government monopoly control as vital. Radio stations are sufficiently cheap to establish that, freed from government restraints on entry, there are likely to be too many of them for the government to be able to control them all.

Beyond the media, what else? Democracy is designed very differently in different places, so it is pointless trying to set out some grand blueprint that all democracies should follow. There is, however, one other aspect of democracy where international standards would help to curtail massive abuse, and that it how money is raised and spent on election campaigning. I grew up in Britain, which has very strict limits both on how money can be raised and on how it can be spent. I used to be amazed by U.S.-style campaign finance, but that was before I looked around. Even before we get to the bottom billion, campaign spending in the new democracies is amazing. Look at Russia. An election campaign costs around four times as much there as it does in the United States, despite Russia's income being only about a tenth of that in America. In relative terms this is forty times the U.S. level of spending. And look at Nigeria. Never mind the presidential campaign there—just to get elected as a senator costs around half a million dollars. With spending like that, no wonder the politics is corrupt. To raise that sort of money candidates have to sell their houses, borrow, and beg, and then if they win they have just four years to recoup their investment.

How is money spent during campaigns? Voters are often literally bribed to support a particular party. Transparency International has studied the various types of bribe: money, food, and clothing. All this obviously detracts from choosing candidates on the basis of their performance. There is no ideal way of financing election campaigns, but surely we can all agree that outright bribery of voters is not acceptable. Probably parliaments should also set some ceilings on contributions, and require some transparency in party finances. This is not a very ambitious agenda, but it would at least get the issue of campaign finance started.

A Charter for Budget Transparency

How governments spend money is at the core of how they function. At present spending by the governments of the bottom billion is often atrocious. Remember the survey tracking spending on health clinics in Chad—99 percent of the money did not reach its intended destination. It is possible to do something about that sort of failure. Practical measures of scrutiny and accountability can make a big difference. Here is a more encouraging story. The heroes are Emmanuel Tumusiime-Mutebile, now governor of the central bank of Uganda, but in the mid-1990s permanent secretary of the Ministry of Finance and Planning, and Ritva Reinikka, a former student of mine. The story begins with Reinikka devising a survey to track public expenditure (the same survey that was done in Chad). She initially devised it for Uganda, where it came up with rather depressing results: only around 20 percent of the money that the Ministry of Finance released for primary schools, other than for teachers' salaries, actually reached the schools. In some societies the government would have tried to suppress information like this, but in Uganda, far from suppressing it, Tumusiime-Mutebile used it as a springboard for action. Obviously, one way would have been to tighten the top-down system of audit and scrutiny, but they had already been trying that and it evidently wasn't working too well. So Tumusiime-Mutebile decided to try a completely different approach: scrutiny from the bottom up. Each time the Ministry of Finance released money it informed the local media, and it also sent a poster to each school setting out what it should be getting. Tumusiime-Mutebile is a practical man who wanted to know if things were working, so three years later he repeated the tracking survey. Now, instead of only 20 percent getting through to the schools, 90 percent was getting through. In state-of-the-art statistical research that analyzed this experiment in detail, Reinikka and her colleague Jakob Svensson were able to demonstrate that the media had been decisive—in this case reports in newspapers. So scrutiny turned 20 percent into 90 percent—more effective than doubling aid and doubling it again. Not that scrutiny and aid are substitutes: if scrutiny can make spending effective, it then becomes more worthwhile to scale up aid.

Tumusiime-Mutebile's strategy of publishing budget releases was taken up by Ngozi Okonjo-Iweala when she became minister of finance in Nigeria in 2003. One of her first acts was to publish the budget releases to the states, month by month. On the first day of publication newspaper circulation spiked: citizens wanted to know what was happening to their money. That and the death threats made her realize she was on the right track.

So a charter on budget processes could usefully specify scrutiny from the bottom up as well as from the top down. There is a third type of scrutiny that comes sideways, so to speak: comparison with peers. I first came across this as a serious strategy for the bottom billion when it was promoted by a young Nigerian academic, Charles Soludo, who at the time was a lowly consultant to the Economic Commission for Africa but is now the reformist governor of the Central Bank of Nigeria and has just been voted Governor of the Year. The idea next surfaced in a process known as the African Peer Review Mechanism, whereby African countries volunteer for self-evaluation, modeled on the OECD. It is also useful within countries, as local governments can be compared against each other and ranked. Public agencies hate such rankings because they generate very effective pressure, both from the humiliation within a peer group and from the anger of users. Of course performance measures can be misleading, but the answer is to make them better.

Each of these three directions of scrutiny can operate ex ante and ex post. Ex ante is about authorization for spending and ex post is about evaluation, such as the tracking surveys. Finally, two very distinct aspects of expenditures need to be scrutinized: their honesty and their efficiency. Reformers usually focus on honesty, but efficiency may be even more important, and its scrutiny requires radically different skills. I think of them as a double hurdle.

A charter for budget scrutiny does not need to be sophisticated. It could just spell out these three directions of scrutiny, the two time frames, and the two criteria. Introducing scrutiny into the societies of the bottom billion will always take courage, but perhaps the existence of an international charter would lower the threshold a little.

A Charter for Postconflict Situations

Probably the situation that presents the greatest scope for an international charter pertinent for the bottom billion is the end of a conflict. Think of Afghanistan, Sudan, and Burundi. Recall that although these situations typically start out with very poor governance and policies, they are highly fluid: change is easy. However, the range of postconflict outcomes is extremely wide. Some countries grow rapidly and maintain peace, while others fall apart again. This range of outcomes is far wider than the normal diversity of country experience. The very diversity suggests that some standards might be useful—if we could bring the worst up closer to the present best, it would make an enormous difference. Standards do not need to be abstract, but can draw upon the experience of what has worked well.

A postconflict charter should include guidance on behavior by donors and the international security regime. Donors should be committed for the decade, not just the first couple of high-glamour years. International security forces should likewise be committed for the long haul. In return, postconflict governments should reduce their own military spending—as we have seen, it is dysfunctional. They should have a transparent budgetary process, so that public power does not translate into private profit. They should include opposition groups in power, for example through decentralization. And they should sort out conflicting and confused property claims quickly. These essential steps could be set out in an international charter. The international community has a very strong interest that postconflict situations should go right, and it puts huge resources into them. Postconflict governments are typically highly reliant upon others, and it is entirely reasonable that they should be, in effect, on probation for that first decade, placed under a set of rules that define the minimum acceptable progress before untrammeled sovereignty can be achieved.

A charter for postconflict situations could also usefully draw on the successful experiences of truth and reconciliation commissions; perhaps the most highly visible one is South Africa's, but there have been others. Neither a vindictive pursuit of victor's justice nor a blanket of forgetfulness is desirable. An international norm would provide a much-needed sense of impartiality, typically lacking when procedures are drawn up ad hoc by whoever holds power in each particular situation. Some postconflict processes have managed a swift drawing of lines that prosecutes some of the major offenders on both sides and gets as much as possible of the rest into the public record.

One aspect of postconflict policy is noticeable by its absence from the above suggestions: that relating to elections. At present, postconflict political evolution is often dominated by elections, which are often imagined to be the key to reestablishing peace. If that is indeed the case, then elections should be a part of the postconflict charter. But are they in fact so important? The team working on this included Anke Hoeffler, Måns Söderbom, and myself. Somewhat laboriously we built a data set on all postconflict experiences—more than sixty of them. We then looked to see what effect elections had on the risk of the reversion to conflict. (This work is new, so it has yet to be properly peer-reviewed.) The issue is contentious. In the world of postconflict studies there are two camps: those who think elections make things better, and those who think they make them worse. Each camp can point to particular elections for which their thesis looks plausible, but they cannot both be right. They can, however, both be wrong. As far as we can see, they are. Elections during the postconflict decade seem to *shift* the risk. In the year before an election the risk of renewed conflict goes sharply down, perhaps because the various groups direct their energies to the electoral contest. In the year after an election the risk goes equally sharply up: presumably whoever has lost the election does not like the result and is inclined to explore other options. So elections may be desirable for all sorts of reasons, but they do not seem to make the society safer. Perhaps as solutions they have been a little overplayed.

A Charter for Investment

The bottom billion need private capital. Even though the world is awash with capital, the poorest countries are failing to attract it and are instead hemorrhaging their own. Remember that a key problem is the lack of reform credibility. Credibility looms large because investment runs up against the time consistency problem that we have repeatedly encountered. Once made, investment is far more difficult and costly to reverse than are policies, and so investors are wary of falling for a policy that looks attractive but is not maintained. The only option that is currently open to individual governments that are committed to reform is the costly and dangerous strategy of revealing their true type by going too far too fast. Can an international charter do better?

What would an investment charter do? It would set out some simple rules to which a government would commit itself in its treatment of investors. Many governments already do this through national charters, but these charters lack credibility for precisely the reasons that there is a problem in the first place. The rules should apply to domestic investors as well as foreign investors, otherwise capital flight would be accentuated. Essentially, a charter would preclude governments from strategies of confiscation.

A government set on confiscation in fact has many options open to it—it does not literally have to confiscate the assets. It can manipulate taxes, the exchange rate, and the prices that public utilities charge. That is, it can use policy instruments that all governments use, but push them into a range that is meant to be ruinous for a given company or industry. This is inevitably a matter of judgment, and so the essence of an effective charter is that there has to be some system of adjudication. Governments of course have their own judicial system, but it is hardly reassuring for investors if their only defense is through the courts of the government that has confiscated their investment. There are two complementary solutions, international arbitration and investor insurance. International arbitration is not an affront to sovereignty. It is simply a recognition that a government may find it very useful to put itself in a position where it has to argue its case before a neutral body rather than be free to ignore its own commitments. The governments that would find such a facility most useful are those that have severe problems of reputation and are trying to live them down. Arbitration has its limits because even if the arbitrator finds in favor of an expropriated company the government may choose to ignore the decision. That is where insurance comes in. Those rich-country governments with companies that have substantial investments abroad long ago established insurance protection for them. In the United States the organization is called the Overseas Private Investment Corporation (OPIC), and in the United Kingdom it is the Export Credits Guarantee Department (ECGD). Obviously, they only provide insurance coverage for their countries' own companies. Eventually, the board of the World Bank established an insurance company that could cater more globally. It is called the Multilateral Investment Guarantee Agency (MIGA). If a firm that has taken out insurance with MIGA is expropriated, then MIGA pays up. It tries to recover the money from the offending government, which often takes years, but the company does not have to worry. Since the bottom-billion countries need private investment and this requires addressing the problem of investor risk, it was entirely appropriate for a global public development agency such as the World Bank to provide this service.

MIGA, however, has one grave shortcoming. MIGA covers only foreign investment, and this creates two major problems. Domestic investors are important—behind them lies all the capital that has left the country, in part because of risk, and needs to be attracted back into the country. And by covering only foreign investors MIGA breaches the level playing field that governments are routinely urged to create for investors. Indeed, if you think about it, it is self-evidently preposterous that a global public institution should be favoring foreign investors over the citizens of low-income countries. The recent Commission for Africa proposed that MIGA should be opened up.

The world nearly got a charter on investment. In the late 1990s the OECD proposed a Multilateral Agreement on Investment. The OECD probably was not the ideal institution to promulgate such a charter because it does not have developing-country representation and so can easily be portrayed as merely serving the interests of rich countries. However, given the extreme shortage of agencies in a position to overcome the free rider problem associated with such a charter, the OECD was decidedly better than nothing—but that is what we have ended up with. The OECD was opposed by two groups. One was the governments of the bottom billion that are run by crooks and populists. Leaders as notorious as Idi Amin, Mobutu Sese Seko, and Robert Mugabe have depended upon not being differentiated from those who are genuinely trying to develop their countries. The whole point of an investment charter is for newly reforming governments to be able to signal their separation from this nefarious crew more cheaply than through the signaling strategies that are presently available. While this source of opposition was inevitable yet could have been faced down, the other source was not inevitable but proved decisive. The development NGOs lobbied against the Multilateral Agreement on Investment in much the same way that, as you are about to see, the British charity Christian Aid has more recently lobbied against African trade liberalization. This was because the NGOs misread what the charter was about. They saw it as rich countries ganging up on poor countries to protect their capital investments, and did not acknowledge the reality that in the bottom billion there was no capital to protect because the risks had frightened investors off. An investment charter, and indeed the World Trade Organization (WTO), can provide the governments of the bottom billion with a means of locking themselves into the commitments that they choose to make. In the language of economics the general concept is termed "commitment technologies." For the bottom billion these technologies are chronically lacking, and the resulting credibility problem is debilitating for private investment. Without radically higher private investment the reforming countries will not be able to reach middle-income status but will linger in limbo and risk falling back into one of the traps. By posing the problem as that of a grasping rich world imposing its rules on a weak poor world, the NGOs conjured up a satisfyingly simple moral struggle in which they could campaign. But it was a fantasy world that, sad to say, did a disservice to the very people the NGOs are passionately trying to help. It was the headless heart in action.

Changing Our Laws, Promulgating International Charters: Global Public Goods

Changing our laws and promulgating international charters are global public goods. This is a grandiose way of saying that providing them is going to be problematic. Global public goods are grossly undersupplied because nobody has much interest in providing them. Being good for everybody, they face the ultimate free-rider problem. The real problem, therefore, is not that of not knowing what to do but getting around to doing it. I will return to that problem in Part 5.

CHAPTER 10

Trade Policy for Reversing Marginalization

GENERALLY, I DO NOT MUCH CARE for rich-country wallowing in guilt over development. I find it contrived, and it diverts attention from a practical agenda. Citizens of the rich world are not to blame for most of the problems of the bottom billion; poverty is simply the default option when economies malfunction. However, I am now going to pin some blame on citizens of the rich world, who must take responsibility for their own ignorance about trade policy and for its consequences. You personally may be well informed about trade, but if so, you are in a minority; in general rich-country electorates are deeply misinformed. Here is an example of the consequences.

In fall 2004, Christian Aid—about the most trusted of the British charities—started a huge and expensive advocacy campaign about trade policy for the countries at the bottom. Under the slogan "Free Trade: Some People Love It," a capitalist, literally depicted as a pig, sat on top of an African peasant woman. That a Christian charity should be peddling the crudest images of Marxism may strike you as a little strange and is an interesting line of inquiry, but this ideological cross-dressing is not my point. The key thing is that this message was grotesquely wrong. Trade policy is the area of economics least well understood by the NGO world.

In the fall of 2005 Christian Aid stepped up its advertising campaign—trade advocacy, it said, was its biggest issue. It claimed that Africa's rather modest reductions in its trade barriers had already cost the region an astonishing $272 billion. This estimate, proclaimed the Christian Aid Web site, came from work it had itself commissioned from "an expert in econometrics" whose work had then been reviewed by "a panel of academic experts." I was somewhat surprised by this, so I e-mailed Christian Aid, and they duly sent me the study and the composition of the expert panel. Christian Aid, I concluded, was being a little economical with the truth—surely somewhat unfortunate in one of our most respected charities. The "expert" they had commissioned turned out to be a young man at the School of Oriental and African Studies, the only economics department in Britain that is solidly Marxist. He had, as far as I could tell from Google Scholar, never published an article on trade, but had previously written an unpublished paper denouncing international trade policies. However, I was reassured to see that his paper was issued by a group called CEPR, which I took as the acronym for the Centre for Economic Policy Research, probably the most respected economics think tank in Britain. You have to be a fellow of the CEPR to issue one of their working papers, and they set high standards. But then I discovered that the CEPR that had issued his paper was not the internationally renowned London group but the Center for Economic and Policy Research, a little outfit in the United States. I do not imagine for a moment that there was any deliberate misrepresentation involved; it just misled me. And, after all, there was the "academic panel." Unfortunately, this turned out to be two gentlemen whom the author himself had chosen and who were not noted for their expertise on international trade. So here was the largest charity campaign in the United Kingdom spending many thousands of pounds donated by Christians around the country who had given their money to what they imagined was an organization that they could trust beyond question, and the campaign was based on this unpublished paper. I decided that it was time to subject this paper to proper scrutiny. As it happens, I did my doctorate on international trade; though I would not claim to be one of the real experts, at least I know who they are. So I sent it to three of the world's leading experts on international trade: Jagdish Bhagwati, professor at Columbia University, Kofi Annan's trade advisor, and probably the greatest living expert on international trade; Tony Venables, whose work you have already come across in Chapter 6 and who is professor of international economics at the London School of Economics and currently also chief economist at the Department for International Development, Britain's aid agency; and finally David Greenaway, a professor at the University of Nottingham, head of its Globalization Centre, and editor of the journal *The World Economy*. They all decided that the study was deeply misleading. In the end, we sent a joint letter to the *Financial Times*, issuing a warning.

I do not know whether this is simply an example of the headless heart. Trade policy is unusually difficult for people to understand, and Christian Aid may well not have done sufficient homework. It may instead be that its advocacy department has been infiltrated by Marxists, as briefly happened to the British Labour Party in the 1980s. The most depressing explanation I have heard came from an expert at the Department of Trade and Industry, who had better stay nameless. His account was: "They know it's crap but it sells the T-shirts." As I write, it is too early to tell which situation it is—confused Christians, infiltrating Marxists, or corporate marketing executives—so you will need to consult the group's Web site and judge for yourself.

Another government insider who had also better remain anonymous told me that the politicians were too scared of Christian Aid to dare to contradict it. Clare Short, a soon-to-retire member of Parliament and a former secretary of state for international development, was the only one with the guts to take them on, he said, and she's gone. So, unlikely as it seems, it is the NGOs that now have power without responsibility. And that is because the general public is ignorant of trade policy but trusts Christian Aid to get it right. The question, then, is what a responsible NGO should be campaigning for.

Rich-Country Trade Policy Is Part of the Problem

As everyone knows, there are some indefensible aspects of OECD trade policy. The least defensible, from the perspective of both OECD citizens and people in developing countries, is probably the protection of agriculture. We waste our own money subsidizing the production of crops that then close off opportunities for people who have few alternatives. When U.S. and European Union trade negotiators jointly proposed that instead of the OECD lowering these production subsidies poor countries might shift to other activities, I personally felt they had crossed the line beyond which the normal diplomatic act of lying for your country becomes too shaming to accept. The U.S. South really does have alternatives to cotton: its cotton growers live in the most bountiful economy on earth. But cotton growers in Chad? Another dysfunctional aspect of rich-country trade policy is tariff escalation: the tariffs on processed materials are higher than on the unprocessed materials. This makes it harder for the countries of the bottom billion to diversify their exports by processing their raw materials before exporting them. It hurts us and impedes the development of countries that are already facing enough impediments.

These are examples of "policy incoherence," where one policy works against another. It is stupid to provide aid with the objective of promoting development and then adopt trade policies that impede that objective. The reason this happens is that trade policy is *negotiated*. The essence of the World Trade Organization (and of its predecessor organization, the General Agreement on Tariffs and Trade, or GATT) is that the reduction in our trade restrictions is something that we concede only in return for others doing likewise. The countries at the bottom played no part in GATT— mostly they were not even members. But when the WTO was formed in 1995 they all joined, for being in this club meant belonging to the modern world. However, they have virtually no role in an organization that is designed for bargaining. The countries at the bottom have no markets of any interest to the rest of the world, and so their high trade restrictions are also of no interest.

Bottom-Billion Trade Barriers Are Also Part of the Problem

What about trade protection on the part of the bottom billion themselves? Their own individual markets are tiny and stagnant, so focusing on the domestic market, which is all that protection can achieve, is going to get nowhere. Despite this, trade protection has been the ostensible strategy of bottom-billion governments for forty years, although its main motivation for protection was probably not strategic at all. The high tariffs induced a high-cost, parasitic industry that realized its profits depended upon lobbying rather than on productive efficiency. Globally, we now know what produces productivity growth in manufacturing: it is competition. Firms hate competition because it forces them into painful changes, and painful change is what generates productivity growth. Bottom-billion firms have faced very little competition. They have been protected from external competition by trade barriers, and from internal competition because the domestic market is often too small to support more than one or two firms in an activity. The quiet life that bottom-billion firms have enjoyed has been paid for by ordinary people, who have faced prices inflated above world levels by protection. That is what protection means. The quiet life has shown up in the rate of productivity growth. In bottom-billion manufacturing the rate has been around zero, in contrast to the global trend of rapid progress. Gradually, over the past two decades governments have been coaxed and cajoled into reducing trade barriers. Inevitably, when exposed to external competition these unviable activities curl up and die. I am not, however, an enthusiast for "big bang" trade liberalization: where there is some hope that firms can become globally competitive it may be better to draw their feet gradually closer to the fire than to push them into sudden death. Trade liberalization has got parasitic firms off the backs of ordinary people, but it has not enabled other activities to flourish. For that governments need to change a whole range of policies that between them determine firms' costs.

Why do the governments of the bottom billion typically adopt high trade barriers? Partly because they are one of the key sources of corruption. That's why political reformers such as Marc Ravalomanana in Madagascar, Emmanuel Tumusiime-Mutebile in Uganda, and Ngozi Okonjo-Iweala in Nigeria all made trade liberalization a priority. The corruption generated by trade restrictions works on both grand and petty scales. On the grand scale, governments confer protection on the businesses owned by their friends and relations, or ones that pay for the privilege. At the petty level, actually running the system of protection day to day can be lucrative. Becoming a customs officer is about the best job you can possibly get in these countries. For example, in Madagascar, to become a customs officer you have to go to the school that trains them. So getting into the school is a passport to prosperity. The bribe to get a place is fifty times the country's per capita annual income. That tells you all you need to know about the customs service in Madagascar. The vice president of Nigeria used to be a customs officer. He had talents and so was offered promotion, but he turned it down; one can imagine why.

The enthusiasm of the villains for the opportunities for corruption that trade restrictions constitute, and the consequent struggle of reformers to reduce barriers, is misread by NGOs such as Christian Aid. Seeing everything through the spectrum of rich countries oppressing poor countries, these agencies spend charitable donations opposing the reduction in African trade barriers. Lenin had a phrase for those in the West who supported him without understanding his true intent: "useful idiots." Today's useful idiots campaign for trade barriers.

Aid Worsens the Problem of Trade Barriers

Although Christian Aid wants Africa to maintain high trade barriers, of course it also wants a big increase in aid. These two positions are disastrously incompatible. Extra aid needs to be accompanied by African trade liberalization or it could even increase poverty. Aid can only be used for imports. I know this sounds a bit odd: aid is supposed to be paying for schools and suchlike. But aid is foreign exchange—dollars, pounds, euros. If governments choose to spend this aid on schools, they have to sell the foreign exchange to generate local currency. People buy the foreign exchange in order to pay for imports. So aid is valuable only to the extent that people want to buy imports. If imports are banned or have very high tariffs imposed on them, then the demand for foreign exchange will be low and the aid will not buy much schooling. It gets worse. Other than through aid, societies pay for imports through exports. Exporters earn foreign exchange and sell it to people who want to buy imports. So importers have the choice between getting their foreign exchange from exporters and getting it from aid. Put another way, aid is in competition with exporters. More aid means less need for exports and so exporters earn less. The mechanism that generates this effect is the exchange rate: aid appreciates the exchange rate, making a dollar earned by an exporter worth less in terms of local currency. Exporters get squeezed as a result, and some go out of business. This is the problem of Dutch disease once again. Dutch disease is rather worrying for aid enthusiasts. If a big increase in aid ruins export competitiveness, then inadvertently it accentuates the very problem that the bottom-billion countries need to put right—making new export activities competitive.

Fortunately, trade liberalization is one of the remedies for Dutch disease. Extra aid increases the *supply* of imports, and so a matching increase in the *demand* for imports is needed. Only with a matching increase in demand are exporters not disadvantaged by the extra aid. Trade liberalization increases the demand for imports by making them cheaper without the need to appreciate the exchange rate: the taxes imposed on imports are reduced. How much trade liberalization is needed? That depends upon what the aid is used for. If the aid is used to buy foreign expertise, it directly increases the need for foreign exchange, as foreign experts are paid in dollars. But if the aid is used to pay for local schoolteachers, then it has little direct effect on the need for foreign exchange, as schoolteachers are paid in local currency and probably don't spend much of their salary on imports. So the sort of social uses that NGOs tend to favor generally require more trade liberalization than the growth-oriented uses such as expertise and infrastructure. Christian Aid should be campaigning for African trade liberalization alongside extra aid. I do not know whether the advocacy people in Christian Aid simply have not understood this connection between aid and trade policy. It is not Christian Aid's fault if trade liberalization doesn't sell T-shirts as well as depictions of capitalist pigs do, but profiting from popular misconceptions *is* their fault.

What Are the Answers?

Is Fair Trade the Answer?

The fair trade campaign attempts to get higher prices for some of the bottom billion's current exports, such as coffee. The price premium in fair trade products is a form of charitable transfer, and there is evidently no harm in that. But the problem with it, as compared with just giving people the aid in other ways, is that it encourages recipients to stay doing what they are doing—producing coffee. A key economic problem for the bottom billion is that producers have not diversified out of a narrow range of primary commodities. Raising their prices (albeit infinitesimally, since fair trade is such a small component of demand) makes it harder for people to move into other activities. They get charity as long as they stay producing the crops that have locked them into poverty.

Is Regional Integration the Answer?

For forty years the politically correct solution to bottom-billion trade problems has been regional integration. The success of the European Community as an economic free trade area (technically a customs union) added political impetus to a strategy that was already attractive. Countries could keep high barriers against rich countries but remove them against each other. There are so many fallacies in this approach that it is a question of where to start. But the politics were indeed magical. So attractive were regional integration schemes that they proliferated. In fact, the world now has more regional trade schemes than countries, so some countries must be in many of them; the typical African country is in four arrangements, often incompatible ones. Why have they been so popular? Well, presidents could get in their jets, meet up with some of the neighbors and sign a trade protocol, set up a regional secretariat to which they appointed their friends, and fly out again, having garnered lots of publicity.

Such schemes have not accomplished much, however. One reason is that even in the best-case scenario, the resulting markets remain tiny. A famous statistic is that the whole of sub-Saharan Africa has an economy about the size of Belgium's. A second reason is that if you combine a number of poor, slow-growing individual economies, you have a poor, slow-growing regional economy. Trade is really generated by differences, and the big opportunity for low-income countries is to trade with rich countries, harnessing the advantage of their cheap labor. Within a group of poor countries there simply are not sufficient differences to generate much trade. Worse, the differences that do exist between poor countries will get reinforced rather than reduced. The model of the European Community is unfortunately deeply misleading.

Recall that Europe's great success has been convergence: the poorer countries, such as Portugal and Ireland, have caught up with the richer countries. Free trade within Europe has been equalizing and will continue to be with the recent enlargement of the EU. Tony Venables discovered, on the other hand, that regional integration between poor countries generates *divergence* instead of convergence. The reason for this is that regional schemes, whether between rich countries or poor countries, benefit those member countries that have characteristics closest to the global average. In a rich-country club, the member closest to the global average is the poorest member; in a poor-country club, the member closest to the global average is the richest. So in the rich-country clubs the poorest member gains (convergence) while in the poor-country clubs the richest member gains (divergence). Why does a regional scheme benefit those countries closest to the global average? Think of the European Union. Its common external tariff keeps out labor-intensive goods from poor countries. This creates opportunities for the countries within the EU that have the cheapest labor, which are the poorest member countries. The middle, with relatively cheap labor, is protected from the very cheap-labor extreme. Now think it through for a scheme among the bottom billion. The common external tariff keeps out skill-intensive goods from rich countries. This creates opportunities for those countries within the club that have the most skills, which are the richest members. The relatively skill-abundant middle is protected from the very skill-abundant extreme.

Where regional trade schemes have been effective in the bottom billion we see these forces for divergence at work. In West Africa, Burkina Faso lost market share to the local leaders, Senegal and Côte d'Ivoire. In East Africa, Uganda and Tanzania lost market share to local leader Kenya. Of course, the countries that lose out don't like it. In East Africa the experiment of regional free trade ended with a complete closure of borders and an intraregional war. More commonly, the arrangements never get implemented. For regional schemes among the bottom billion to make sense, the external tariff has to be low. A high external tariff implies that ordinary people in Tanzania and Burkina Faso are subsidizing inefficiently high-cost industry in Kenya and Senegal. These transfers are regressive and pointless. Only low external tariffs can keep them at manageable levels.

Good access to neighboring markets is vital for landlocked countries without resources—countries such as Burkina Faso and Uganda most surely need regional integration. But they should not have to pay for this market access by large transfers to richer neighbors. Uganda has good and plentiful agricultural land. It should be feeding Kenya. When the Kenyan government permits the imports, it does just that. But Uganda has no power over Kenya. Daniel arap Moi, president of Kenya from 1978 to 2002, was famously in hock to local business interests. At one stage some Kenyan businessmen took a speculative position on food grains, stocking warehouses in anticipation of higher prices. But because of imports from Uganda, prices didn't go up. The businessmen lobbied President Moi, and sure enough, he imposed a total ban on food imports from Uganda. So ordinary Kenyans had to pay more for their food, and ordinary Ugandans lost the chance to earn a living through exports. Only President Moi's business friends were happy. I expect they showed their gratitude. I met Moi just after he had taken this decision, and challenged him on it. He told me that he had done it for the Kenyan poor, but one of his aides was sufficiently irritated by this answer to take me aside after the meeting and tell me the truth. So regional integration is a good idea, but not behind high external barriers.

Part of the Answer: Export Diversification

Manufacturing in the bottom billion is in decline. Thirty years of protection created a parasite with stagnant productivity, and a decade of modest liberalization has merely reduced its size. How could manufacturing get on a productivity escalator?

For over a decade I have been part of a large network of scholars, Industrial Surveys of Africa, that has been studying African manufacturing. The group has been trying to discover what would make firms grow. We have looked, for example, at how firms cope with a high-risk environment, at why they invest so little, and at the effect of credit constraints. One of our most striking findings concerned exporting. African firms can and do export, but not many of them are involved. Those firms that are involved experience rapid growth of productivity. As usual with such a correlation, the problem is to sort out the direction of causality. Is it that the rare firms with rapid productivity growth are the ones able to export? (In which case, so what?) Or is it that exporting induces productivity growth? There have been similar studies for firms in the United States and for emerging market economies such as China, but ours is, I think, the only one for bottom-billion economies. For firms in the United States, exporting has no effect on productivity growth. This is not surprising, since firms can learn as much from competing to sell products in Kansas as they can from selling them in France. The same turns out to be true of China. Evidently, the Chinese market is sufficiently large and competitive that companies have to keep getting more productive in order to survive. But Africa is a different story. There, exporting really does appear to raise productivity. Domestic markets are too small to support much competition, and so learning from exporting is differentially powerful. We found it was a big effect: whereas the norm for African manufacturing was stagnant productivity, exporting got a firm on a productivity escalator.

So if Africa, and by extension the other bottom-billion economies, are to get a dynamic manufacturing sector, it is more likely to come from breaking into export markets than from going back to the years of cozy domestic monopolies. The problem is how to get firms over that initial hump of competitiveness and enable them to get on the escalator.

How to Get Export Diversification Started: Protection from Asia

The bottom billion do need some helpful OECD trade policies, but they are not fair trade, nor could they be described as trade justice. And they certainly don't fit with Christian Aid's Marxist slogan. The bottom billion need to diversify their exports into labor-using manufactures and services, the sort of things that Asia is already doing. Remember that this is the problem—having broken into these markets, low-income Asia now has the huge advantage of established agglomerations where costs are lower than for those just starting up elsewhere. When Asia broke into these markets it did not have to compete with established low-cost producers, because it was the first on the block. For the bottom billion to break into these markets they need temporary protection *from Asia.*

What this means is that goods and services exported from the bottom billion to the rich world markets would pay lower tariffs than the same goods coming from Asia. However you package this, it is hard to get the word "justice" or "fair" into the frame. Privileging the bottom billion against low-income Asia is not just or fair; a more accurate word might be "expedient." Without such a pump-priming strategy, the bottom billion are probably doomed to wait until Asia becomes rich and is at a substantial wage disadvantage against the bottom billion. Even with high Asian growth, it will take several decades to open up a wage gap that is wide enough to spur firms to relocate. Only around 16 percent of the cost of labor-intensive goods is, in fact, wages. So if bottom-billion wages were one-sixteenth of

Asia's, this would provide only a 15 percent cost advantage. You then set the meter ticking on other cost disadvantages, such as transport costs, law enforcement, corruption, electricity, and availability of skilled labor and business services. You soon get to 15 percent. Remember, the Asia-OECD wage gap grew very wide before Asia became competitive with the OECD.

It is, of course, inconceivable that the OECD would impose new tariffs on Asia that protected the bottom billion in OECD markets, nor should they. Rather, they should remove tariffs against the bottom billion where they already have tariffs against Asia. One vital implication of this is that the strategy is urgent. World tariff levels are falling. The WTO is in the process of negotiating mutual tariff reductions between the successful developing countries, which clearly have a lot to bargain with, and the OECD. This is its core business, and over the next decade it will probably succeed. So by around 2015, OECD tariffs against Asia will not be high enough for there to be much scope for protecting the bottom billion. We must use this policy opportunity now because it will not be available later. However, the same feature that makes the strategy urgent also makes it both acceptable and potent. The policy is urgent because tariffs against Asia are temporary. This makes protection for the bottom billion much more acceptable for Asia—the policy will phase out. Indeed, it might be to Asia's advantage. Once OECD protectionist interests realize that their lobbying is helping the bottom billion rather than themselves, they will be less inclined to oppose the liberalization that Asia is so keen to see happen. Temporariness also increases potency. If governments in the bottom billion know that they have a window of opportunity of only a few years to break into OECD markets, they are more likely to make the complementary policy changes than if they thought the opportunity would always be there.

Is temporary protection for the bottom billion against Asia in OECD markets politically infeasible? Definitely not—in fact, we are already doing it. The United States has a scheme called the African Growth and Opportunity Act (AGOA), which does just that. Products from Africa enter the U.S. market duty free. The EU has a scheme called Everything but Arms (EBA) that is supposed to do the same for access to the European market. And in Singapore in December 2005 rich-country governments from all the OECD countries committed to freer access for the least developed countries. If we are already doing it, why the fuss? Because these schemes don't work. This is not because they are a bad idea but because the devil is in the details and the details are wrong, probably deliberately—such schemes were designed not to be effective but to appease lobbies. AGOA got adopted because sixty thousand African Americans sent letters to their congressional representatives supporting it.

So what details matter? The first and foremost are the rules of origin (ROOs). In modern production inputs are brought in from around the world and assembled, and the result is exported. ROOs are about those imported inputs, where they can be from, and how much value they can constitute relative to what is produced. ROOs are not arcane. If the economies of the bottom billion really could export anything to the rich countries free of import restrictions, with no ROOs, then all China's exports to us would pass through bottom-billion countries to have little labels added saying "Made in X." They would then come in duty free. It would help China, and incidentally it would help us, but it wouldn't do much for the bottom billion. But at present we are at the other extreme: the ROOs are too restrictive. If a Ugandan fishing boat on Lake Victoria employs a Kenyan, the fish are not eligible for the EU scheme. The same problem was initially true of AGOA, but a special waiver was added. So even if a Kenyan garment manufacturer uses cheap Asian cloth, the garments can now be imported into the United States. As a result, AGOA has increased African apparel exports by over 50 percent, whereas EBA has been totally ineffective. ROOs can be fine-tuned to make preferential access either effective or useless.

Another detail that matters is the time scale. AGOA grants the special waiver for only one year at a time, and AGOA itself is only guaranteed for three years. This is simply too short a period for firms to make investment decisions based on the market access that AGOA provides. For example, textile firms in Madagascar are now highly profitable exporting to the United States, but they don't expand because they do not know what is going to happen. A longer horizon would be a different matter. If aid is targeting the Millennium Development Goals for 2015, then so should trade policy. The EU scheme certainly doesn't suffer from a short horizon; in fact, it appears to be intended for eternity. But that is about how long it would take firms to understand the documentation—the scheme is massively complicated, and many firms are simply not bothering to use it.

A final important detail is the countries that are included. EBA is confined to the least-developed countries, so Somalia and Liberia are in, but Senegal, Ghana, and Kenya are excluded. AGOA is more inclusive. Confining the arrangements to the least developed superficially sounds well focused but is actually idiotic. Which African countries stand the better chance of breaking into the global markets for manufactures, those like Somalia or those like Ghana? It's the headless heart again, well-meaning gestures rather than well-analyzed actions.

What is needed is one simple scheme—the same scheme across the OECD—with more generous rules of origin, pan-African coverage, and a 2015 phase-out. The details of the scheme need to be sufficiently flexible that they can be adjusted until it works. The intention should be to get the bottom billion into new export markets.

The Other Part of the Answer: Rethinking the Bottom Billion in the WTO

What are the countries of the bottom billion doing in the WTO? It is the successor organization to the GATT, and its basis is reciprocal bargains: I open my market to you if you open your market to me. It is not an international organization in the same sense as, say, the World Bank, the IMF, or the United Nations Development Programme. It does not have resources to disburse to countries, nor an objective that its staff must achieve with such resources. It is not a purposive organization but rather a marketplace. The WTO secretariat is there merely to set up the stalls each day, sweep the floor each evening, and regulate the opening hours. What happens is determined by the bargaining. This made some sense when the bargaining was between the United States and the European Union. Over the years, U.S.-EU trade in manufactures became virtually free of restrictions. The WTO brought in the emerging developing countries: India, Brazil, China, and Indonesia, which have a lot to offer both to each other and to rich countries in terms of reduced trade barriers. In return they can negotiate better access to rich-country markets. But the markets of the bottom billion are so tiny that even if their governments were prepared to reduce trade barriers, this would not confer any bargaining power on them. If the U.S. government decides that the political gains from protecting cotton growers outweigh the political cost of making American taxpayers finance a hugely expensive farm bill, the offer of better access to the market in

Chad is not going to make much difference. So far, the WTO has functioned badly. The present round of trade negotiations was termed a "development round," but such labels really have no possibility of content in an organization designed for bargaining. You might as well label tomorrow's trading on eBay a "development round." Trade negotiators are there to get the best deal for their own country, defined in terms of the least opening of the home market for the maximum opening of others. The countries of the bottom billion joined the WTO hoping to receive transfers in some shape or form, just as they do in the other international organizations such as the World Bank, the IMF, and the United Nations. But the WTO is simply not set up to do this. As long as it is merely a marketplace for bargaining, the bottom billion have no place in it. Their only possibility of power is to threaten the legitimacy of the whole organization. This they have already done, to the point of bringing the round to the brink of failure. The way out of this is for the WTO to add a transfer role to its bargaining role. By this I do not mean a transfer of money. It would be absurd to turn the WTO into yet another aid agency, as there are too many already. By a transfer I mean an *unreciprocated* reduction in trade barriers against the bottom billion: a gift, not a deal. I think that the secretariat of the WTO should be charged with negotiating such a gift as the first phase of each round. The World Bank evolved in an analogous way. Originally, the World Bank was a mutual assistance organization: the International Bank for Reconstruction and Development (IBRD). It issued bonds on the New York market, and lent them on at a small premium to countries that were sufficiently creditworthy. This was of no assistance to low-income countries since they were too risky to be borrowers, so the Bank added a new role: the International Development Association (IDA). Unlike IBRD, which has never cost rich countries a single cent, IDA is a transfer. Every three years the secretariat of the World Bank goes around to the governments of rich countries persuading them to put money into IDA. How much each gives depends upon how good each wants to look relative to the other contributors. The Bank then distributes the funds. So the Bank evolved by adding a transfer role targeted on low-income countries to what was originally a mutual assistance role for richer countries. That is what should happen to the WTO. The secretariat could work on an unreciprocated trade offer, just as World Bank staff have learned how to run an IDA round. The essential step is to quantify the trade concessions offered by each rich country into a common unit—say, expected additional bottom-billion exports. Once concessions are quantified, they can be compared. Then the pressure starts. Why is Japan offering so little relative to Europe? Why is the United States offering no more this round than it did last round? That is the reality of how IDA has worked, and the WTO could do the same. Only once the transfer round was concluded would the bargaining round be permitted to start, and this would put pressure on the rich countries to make acceptable offers. But only once the bargaining round was concluded would the transfer round come into effect, and this would put pressure on the bottom billion to facilitate the bargaining process rather than wreck it. Further, if the bottom billion wanted more than they had received at the end of the transfer round, they would have to get it through bargaining. The two contrasting cultures of transfers and deals would not be confused, as is currently the problem.

Part 5

*The Struggle for the
Bottom Billion*

CHAPTER 11

An Agenda for Action

WE HAVE BEEN THROUGH the costs that the countries of the bottom billion are inflicting on themselves, on each other, and on us. I have tried to put some numbers on the cost of a civil war and the cost of a failing state. They are big numbers. But really it is not necessary to be that sophisticated. I have a little boy who is six. I do not want him to grow up in a world with a vast running sore—a billion people stuck in desperate conditions alongside unprecedented prosperity.

And stuck they will be. Clearly there are brave people within these societies who are struggling to achieve change. It is important to us that these people win their struggle, but the odds are currently stacked against them. We have been through the traps: conflict, natural resources, being landlocked, bad governance. They have kept these countries stagnant for forty years, and I do not see much reason for the next couple of decades to be very different. Will globalization improve the situation? We have been through what it is likely to do for the countries at the bottom. Trade is more likely to lock them into natural resource dependence than to open new opportunities, and the international mobility of capital and skilled workers is more likely to bleed them of their scanty capital and talent than to provide an engine of growth.

If the world is like that in two decades, then, given my profession, my son is going to ask me what I did to avoid it. It has been easy for me to do something: I have written this. But do not think that just because your work is unconnected with development you are off the hook. You are a citizen, and citizenship carries responsibilities. In the 1930s the world sleepwalked into the avoidable catastrophe of World War II because electorates in the United States and Europe were too lazy to think beyond the populist recipes of isolationism and pacifism. These mistakes led to the slaughter of their children. It is the responsibility of all citizens to prevent us from sleepwalking into another avoidable catastrophe that our children would have to face.

And avoidable it is. In this book we have discussed four instruments: aid, security, laws and charters, and trade. Each of these has some bite, yet at present we are using the first quite badly and the three others scarcely at all. Why have the governments of rich countries been so incompetent?

Electorates get what they deserve. Popular thinking on development is fogged by lazy images and controversies: "Globalization will fix it" versus "They need more protection," "They need more money" versus "Aid feeds corruption," "They need democracy" versus "They're locked in ethnic hatreds," "Go back to empire" versus "Respect their sovereignty," "Support their armed struggles" versus "Prop up our allies." These polarizations are untenable, and I hope that you have picked up some sense of how quantitative research on these issues challenges them.

It is now time to pull it all together. In Part 2 we went through the traps, and in Part 4 we went through the instruments. It is now time to relate the instruments to the traps. Not everything is appropriate everywhere. Trap by trap, what combination of instruments is likely to be most effective?

The other key question concerns who is going to make all this happen. Since there is no world government, what is the realistic balance of actions between the rich countries and the bottom-billion societies themselves? Which actions need to be done cooperatively, and how might that happen? Given that even within each group coordination is so difficult, what is the minimum that we can get away with, and how might it be achieved?

What Needs to Happen?

Let's revisit the traps and see how they can be broken by the instruments we now have.

Breaking the Conflict Trap

The conflict trap has two points of intervention: postconflict and deep prevention. Since around half of all civil wars are postconflict relapses, and since these happen in only a few countries, getting a postconflict intervention to work better is a good place to start. It is particularly pertinent at the moment because there have been a lot of recent peace settlements.

Of the four instruments, I think that in postconflict situations we can more or less forget about trade. Afghanistan isn't going to export anything soon except drugs.

Aid to postconflict societies used to be too little too soon. That is already changing. Donors are learning that postconflict situations take time to get better and that aid is more usefully phased over a decade rather than dumped in a rush. The crushing needs of the early postconflict period collide with government incapacity. One way around this is to deliver the key basic services through the independent service authority model: competing organizations provide the services on the ground while the authority finances and scrutinizes their performance. This would enable donors to coordinate, pooling funds into the authority. They could, of course, coordinate through budget support, but many postconflict governments are just too weak for this to be wise. It will also usually make sense for donors to fund traditional projects to restore infrastructure, but they will need exceptionally substantial supervision both to ensure success and to guard against corruption.

Security in postconflict societies will normally require an external military presence for a long time. Both sending and recipient governments should expect this presence to last for around a decade, and must commit to it. Much less than a decade and domestic politicians are liable to play a waiting game rather than building the peace, and firms are likely to be wary of investing. Much more than a decade and citizens are likely to get restive for foreign troops to leave the country. To be effective, an external presence requires troops with a mandate to fight to preserve the peace, as well as contributing governments willing to accept casualties. In return for this external security guarantee, the postconflict government should be required to radically downsize its own army. It has to learn to rule by consent rather than oppression. While the military should be reduced in size, there is likely to be a need for an expanded police force to deal with a crime wave as the violent diversify from war to crime.

In Chapter 9, I proposed a charter for postconflict governance. International actors have had huge power in postconflict situations and have usually been embarrassed to use it because of accusations of infringing upon sovereignty. The international community has so much at stake in these situations that it has to learn to be comfortable with infringing upon sovereignty. But it is far more acceptable for international actors to impose a previously defined international norm than to invent fresh demands on the hoof as a particular situation deteriorates. It is also far easier for international actors to coordinate around an agreed-upon norm than to try to forge an ad hoc coalition problem by problem.

So in postconflict situations three of the four instruments are really important. Aid has already improved a lot, military intervention is improving (or at least it was until Iraq), and charters are currently far behind. Therefore, the most pressing agenda is getting a charter promulgated.

How about conflict prevention? Prevention requires all four instruments because it comes close to being synonymous with development. Recall that the deep risk factors are low income, slow growth, and dependence upon primary commodities. Thus conflict prevention is really about breaking all of the other traps.

Breaking the Natural Resource Trap

Many of the bottom billion are resource-rich and policy-poor. In these countries providing more finance through aid simply misses the point. Our trade policy doesn't have much potential, either, since these countries are going to find it difficult to diversify their exports because of Dutch disease, regardless of any preferences we might give them. They may well need military assistance from time to time, inasmuch as natural resource wealth makes a country more prone to conflict, but I have covered that one in the preceding section. So the key instrument of intervention is likely to be our own laws and international norms. We need that charter for resource wealth—something like a revised version of the Extractive Industries Transparency Initiative. There is a tendency to dismiss this approach by pointing to some difficult countries in which it is likely to be impotent. When the idea of something like the Extractive Industries Transparency Initiative was first floated, the skeptics often pointed to Angola and said, "Forget it." The recent history of the initiative suggests that this was too pessimistic. Both the Kimberley Process and the Extractive Industries Transparency Initiative show that even very modest steps can get some traction. Nor have the skeptics come up with any better solution. Somehow the colonial fantasy persists that we have hard power. We don't, and we never will. Surely after Iraq the chances of a wealthy country attempting external military intervention to transform a badly governed resource-rich country are zero. We can, however, help to empower the reformers within the societies of the bottom billion—or we can sit on our hands while our oil companies compete with the Chinese in the bribery game. Our public inaction does not mean that the rich world is passive; it means that the powerful forces of globalization continue to side with the political crooks in these societies.

Lifelines for the Landlocked

We do not have instruments that are sufficiently powerful to break the trap of being landlocked with bad neighbors. In the end, the landlocked must depend upon more fortunate neighbors making the most of their opportunities, and so for the landlocked trap to be broken the other traps must be broken first. But there is still much that we can do to mitigate the problem.

Aid—yes, certainly, and on a substantial scale. These countries are going to be poor for a long time, and they will need our money not just to develop but to live decently. However, the aid will need to be provided more effectively than in the past. It would make things much simpler if governance and policies in these countries were sufficiently decent for us to provide money unencumbered. Malawi, Burkina Faso, and Uganda should all be receiving massive budget support because governance is already somewhat reformed in these places. But countries where governance remains debilitating, such as Chad and the Central African Republic, need a different approach, such as governance conditionality and independent service authorities. We should also be giving some aid to the neighbors, earmarked for transport corridors.

Remember that large aid inflows into poor countries increase the risk of a coup d'état, presumably because the army catches the scent of money. Even if the military does not actually mount a coup, the threat of one induces the government to increase the military budget preemptively—and some of the funds for this come from the aid itself. So there is a particular role in these countries for external military guarantees against coups. We could legitimately use these guarantees to reinforce the incentives for decent governance. A government might be given a guarantee only if it subjected itself to the effective scrutiny of its own citizens. In other words, a condition might be that the country should adhere to the international charters on democracy and budget transparency that I proposed in Chapter 9.

Our trade policy does not have that much traction for the development of the landlocked because of the natural barrier of transport costs. However, especially for the countries of the Sahel, which, though landlocked, are close to Europe, air freight offers a potential lifeline into European markets. The key export products are likely to be high-value horticulture, and so European trade policy does matter.

Breaking the Reform Impasse in Failing States

Countries with bad governance and policies do sometimes turn themselves around, but too often it is like waiting for Godot. Reform in these countries has to come from within, and it takes courage. Vested interests can be relied upon to use their power, resources, and ingenuity to oppose change. Although the reformers have truth on their side, truth is just another special interest, and not a particularly powerful one. The villains willing to lie in order to defeat change have an advantage over those constrained by honesty. Reformers do not have it easy.

When Charles Soludo became governor of the Central Bank of Nigeria, his priority was to reform the banking sector, a notorious epicenter of rent seeking. Unsurprisingly, this was not popular with the rent seekers among the banks. They organized a fighting fund of around $2 million to campaign against him. Among other tactics, this enabled them to buy allies in the media. Charles did not have $2 million to oppose them; he just had guts and intelligence and the right arguments. As I write, he seems to have won, closing and merging sixty-four banks. Reform is tough, but it can triumph.

The day after President Mwai Kibaki replaced the rent-seeking Daniel arap Moi in Kenya in 2002, ordinary Kenyan citizens frog-marched police officers who demanded the usual bribes to their own police stations to be arrested. People believed that change was at last possible. President Kibaki brought in John Githongo, who had headed the Kenyan branch of Transparency International, as his advisor on fighting corruption. However, once given access to the books, the new team realized the daunting nature of the political problem they faced. The Kenya African National Union (KANU), the former governing party, had over its years of corruption built up a war chest of around $1 billion, naturally held abroad and standing ready to be used in future campaigns. When the scale of what they were up against became apparent, some voices in the new team wanted to emulate the KANU strategy of grand corruption. The British high commissioner was so dismayed by what he witnessed about the misuse of aid money that he spoke out about the villains "vomiting it up" in their greed. In the ensuing struggle for the heart of the new government John Githongo resigned; the story of his struggle must await his telling. Seven months later, in December 2005, the government was defeated in a referendum. The future of reform in Kenya is still not without hope, but now it looks far less promising than at the moment of KANU's defeat.

Kwesi Botchwey, the finance minister who was critical to the turnaround in Ghana during the 1980s, managed to secure the promise of aid from a donor meeting in Paris. When he returned from his trip he rather expected to be greeted by his colleagues in government as a hero, as the situation in the country had become desperate. Instead, they were intensely hostile. He gradually realized that this was because they assumed that he had personally pocketed the money and were jealous. Eventually he quit when President Rawlings' nephew single-handedly smashed the national budget.

Two of these three brave men are currently exiles. The third has placed his family in Europe due to death threats. What we are called upon to do is the safe task of making it easier for such people to win their struggle. Aid can most surely help, but it can also hinder, and so it should be offered intelligently. In Chapter 7, I set out the new evidence on when aid helps reform and when it hinders reform. Intelligent aid would require a substantial reorganization of how technical assistance is delivered. There will, however, surely be resistance in the agencies.

How about military intervention in assisting turnarounds? I think that it is evident that after Iraq even the most ghastly dictators are safe from external military intervention: far from setting a precedent, it has drawn a line. Regime change is going to have to rely on other means. Guarantees against coups might come in handy during turnarounds, but that is probably as far as it goes.

In regard to trade policy, it is a bit premature in these early reform environments to look to export diversification as a big driver of growth. New exports are more likely to get going after governance and policies have been transformed rather than during the process of change. However, a credible prospect of diversification, based on successes in neighboring countries, would probably help to sustain reform.

How about our laws and international norms? Here, I think, are our important missed opportunities. Our laws are going to be critical in reining in corruption. International charters can provide reformers both with an instrument with which to berate poor governance and with a goal around which to unite. That is why international charters will be opposed.

Breaking Out of Limbo

Finally, how about limbo? Some of the coastal, resource-scarce countries managed during the 1990s to break out of the traps, but it was too late: China and India were already established on the block in global markets, making the entry of latecomers much harder. How can we help to shoehorn these countries into the international market? And how can we give newly reforming governments the ability to make their commitments more credible not just to foreigners but to their own people, and so get a surge in private investment?

Remember that aid is a two-edged sword as far as exporting is concerned because of the Dutch disease it generates. The solution to this is a big push: large but temporary aid targeted on raising export infrastructure up to globally competitive levels. It must be temporary because it is only once the aid stops that the Dutch disease problem stops. Like smart technical assistance, big-push aid for exporting will need a transformation within the aid agencies. As for providing a commitment technology for reform, remember that aid in the form of donor conditionality has probably been part of the problem.

It is hard to imagine circumstances in which military intervention would be useful in helping countries break into global markets. Perhaps, however, the catastrophic manner of the political transition to reform in Madagascar might have been averted with more decisive external support for the democratic process. Recall that the defeated president blockaded the port for eight months, killing the export processing zone.

While laws and charters are not directly useful for export diversification, an investment charter would encourage private investment. Not only does rapid growth require a massive increase in private investment, but the new activities that constitute export diversification will need investment.

Evidently, the intervention that is critical for export diversification is trade policy. To my mind it is absolutely vital. Without effective temporary protection against the Asian giants, the countries of the bottom billion will not break into new global markets. Their governments will not even try because they lack belief in themselves and expect to fail. I once suggested to a senior civil servant in the trade ministry of one of the countries of the bottom billion that they focus on new global markets. His response was: "It's like looking at the sun." And remember, with trade preferences the devil is in the details.

Who Should Make It Happen?

There is no world government. That is probably a good thing, but even if you really hope for one, you must face up to the fact that it is not going to happen, at least not in a time frame that is relevant for the problem faced by the bottom billion. Remedying the problems of the bottom billion is a global public good, and so, like the provision of all such public goods, it is going to be difficult.

Mobilizing Changes in Aid Policy

The key obstacle to reforming aid is public opinion. The constituency for aid is suspicious of growth, and the constituency for growth is suspicious of aid. Therefore, using aid strategically to promote growth in the bottom billion is not high on the agendas of politicians. Public opinion drives them into the "I care" photo opportunities that dominate aid. To her immense credit, the former British secretary of state for international development, Clare Short, resisted this temptation, on principle delinking disbursements of aid from her own visits. But she is no longer a strong political actor in this arena.

Aid agencies should become increasingly concentrated in the most difficult environments. That means that they will need to accept more risk, and so a higher rate of failure. They should compensate by increasing their project supervision, which means higher administrative overheads. They should become swift-footed, seizing reform opportunities at an early stage. They should intervene strategically, financing big-push strategies for export diversification. They should introduce governance conditionality. At present the powerful force of popular opinion is driving agencies in precisely the opposite direction. They cannot afford failure. They have to be lean with low administrative expenses. They have to prioritize long-term social objectives rather than short-term opportunities for reform and growth. They have to give unconditional debt relief. This is the fault of ordinary citizens who support vociferous lobbies without bothering to get informed. No aspect of domestic policy is run this badly. The aid agencies are not run by fools; they are full of intelligent people severely constrained by what public opinion permits.

Mobilizing Changes in Military Intervention

Public opinion is also vital for appropriate military intervention. We have had the extremes. One on hand, public opinion has been fed the hype surrounding the initial invasions of Somalia and Iraq—the photographers on the beach in Somalia and "shock and awe" in Iraq. On the other hand, we have seen the cringing feebleness of the United Nations in Rwanda and of the Dutch in Bosnia. Public opinion has to come around to supporting interventions like that of the British in Sierra Leone. If Iraq is allowed to become another Somalia, with the cry "Never intervene," the consequences will be as bad as Rwanda. It would help a lot if countries other than the United States, Britain, and France took up a greater share of the burden. For example, Germany and Japan cannot forever hide behind their history or their absence from the Security Council as an excuse for nonparticipation. They are big countries with an important role to play.

But it is not just the rich countries that need to step up to the plate. The South African government bravely tried to negotiate a settlement in Côte d'Ivoire. It failed, but its ambition was right. I would like to see the leading African states with yet more ambition to bring peace to the continent.

Mobilizing Changes in Our Laws and the Promulgation of International Charters

The big obstacle to changing our own laws is the free rider problem. Remember, each country would rather not act alone and disadvantage its firms. This is the perfect cause for the big international NGOs: with memberships in all the major countries, the NGOs can overcome the free rider problem that constrains each government. In effect, we need an alliance between the NGOs and the OECD, which is the bureaucracy for intergovernmental coordination.

International charters could be powerful forces for improving governance in the bottom billion. Charters would empower the reformers within their societies, and also enable those countries at the early stages of turnaround to lock in change—they would provide an improved commitment technology. Remember that the reformers at present face an acute dilemma: they can only convincingly reveal their type through kamikaze reform strategies. If charters would strengthen reformers and make it easier for reforming governments to distinguish themselves from the villains, then some current governments certainly will be less than enthusiastic about their promulgation. I can already hear accusations of neocolonialism tripping off the tongue of Robert Mugabe. Given this sort of opposition, who is going to champion them?

The promulgation of charters can be done by several processes. We already have many of them. They do not have to be done by the General Assembly of the United Nations, and given Mugabe and his ilk, this route is unlikely. The Extractive Industries Transparency Initiative was launched by the British government. That was enough to get it started, and it has progressed well. Its successor should probably be transferred to one of the international organizations most appropriate for economic management. The boards of these organizations would be appropriate for authorization of something that is voluntary. Similarly, budget processes would lodge most naturally with the IMF, as it already has responsibility for annual consultations with member governments under Article IV of its articles of agreement.

The charter for postconflict governance could be promulgated by the new Peace-Building Commission of the United Nations. Launched in September 2005, it has yet to be given a role, but it is evident that it is seen as a coordinating entity rather than as an implementing agency. A charter would be the ideal way of achieving coordination.

The most difficult charters to place are the political ones, on campaign finance and on checks and balances. The IMF and the World Bank are prohibited by their own rules from involvement in political matters. The United Nations, though obviously political, is subject to the blocking veto of China, which is extremely concerned to head off any suggestion that democracy should be an international standard. One body that could propose political standards would be the European Commission. After all, the EU has explicit standards of democracy that are required for membership. It should not feel squeamish about projecting those standards onto a wider stage than Europe. The promulgation of international standards, applied to its members and more importantly to its prospective members, has been the core business of the European Commission. Its financial role remains puny, with only around 1 percent of European GDP passing through it. It is its regulatory role that gives it significance. Yet to date, in its approach to the bottom billion the Commission has relied exclusively on its aid program. It has not been playing to its strength.

Another possible body to promulgate political standards is the British Commonwealth. After all, the largest country in the Commonwealth is India, which has a longer tradition of democracy than many countries with much higher incomes. India has the prestige to use the Commonwealth to launch a credible charter of minimum standards for the conduct of democracy.

Another possible way of promulgating political standards is through clubs. For example, the four Latin American countries of Mercosur have decided that democracy would be a condition for membership; apparently that helped to avert a coup. The big clubs, such as the African Union, don't work too well in this regard because their membership is indiscriminate. What is needed is small new clubs of the like-minded, adopting standards that set them apart but which are capable of expansion—essentially, open-access clubs of adherence to charters.

Mobilizing Changes in Trade Policy

With trade policy, self-interest meets ignorance and duly manipulates it. Rich-country protectionism masquerades in alliance with antiglobalization romantics and third world crooks. The critical changes in trade policy— temporary protection of the bottom billion from Asia in our markets—are politically difficult not because they threaten interests (they don't) but because they do not fit into any of the current slogans and so don't make it onto the agenda. Protection against Asia is not about justice, fairness, or resisting globalization; rather, it is about pulling the marginalized countries aboard. As we have seen, the development lobbies themselves, notably the big Western NGO charities, often just don't understand trade. It is complicated and doesn't appeal to their publics, so they take the populist line. Even former U.S. president Bill Clinton, that great communicator, said that the hardest idea he ever had to get across to the American electorate was the notion of comparative advantage—that every country can produce something that can be exported to mutual advantage, which is the foundation concept in international trade. Indeed, if you remember what happened during the WTO meeting at Seattle in 1999, when American protectionists allied on the streets with antiglobalization NGOs, you will realize that he failed.

But even more fundamental than this toxic brew is the problem that within the WTO trade policy is determined by national trade representatives who see their role as negotiating a deal. Within this framework there is no scope for using trade policy as an instrument for development. For trade policy to become an instrument of development, ministries of trade have to be ordered to change their priorities from extracting the best bargain to fostering development in the bottom billion. But ordered by whom? This takes us beyond the instrument-by-instrument approach, where we hit four final problems, of coordination and focus.

Problems of Coordination

Within each government the four instruments are lodged in different ministries. Only the development ministries, such as the Department for International Development in the United Kingdom, have development as their objective. And the only instrument that they control is aid. So there is overreliance upon aid, and the development ministries come to define themselves as lobbies for aid rather than as lobbies for development. Success is measured by the size of the aid budget rather than by measures for development. A development minister is much happier talking about how to get aid to 0.7 percent of GDP, the UN target, than about the role of military intervention. Thus the ministry with the nominal responsibility for development has a built-in bias toward one of the four instruments. And because development ministries are pretty low in the government pecking order, they have little sway in interministerial discussions. Expecting the development ministry to persuade the central bank to do something about repatriating corrupt bank deposits is like expecting the general staff to adopt a battle plan drawn up by the catering corps.

The objective of development has to be elevated above the level of the development ministry. Because four different branches of government need to be coordinated, the only level of government likely to be effective is the top. The head of government has to accept development of the bottom billion as a personal priority. Obviously I do not mean that this should be the main priority, for that is unrealistic. Rather, because development requires so much policy coordination it should be recognized as one of those objectives that need to be lodged officially at the top of government. In fact, heads of government are surprisingly keen to take on development as a public objective. Think of the eagerness of George W. Bush to share a platform with Bono. Think of Tony Blair launching the Commission for Africa. What has been lacking is not the commitment so much as the serious content that should follow in its wake. We have had leadership without an adequate agenda, because to date the agenda has been dominated by aid. Bush used his photo opportunity with Bono to announce the Millennium Challenge Account. The Commission for Africa produced a wide-ranging report, but during the ensuing election season it dwindled into a campaign to double aid. A head of government should not be leading an aid campaign; rather, he or she should be forcing policy coordination across the government. That is the head of government's unique role because no one else can do it.

The other coordination problem is between governments. This is the global public-good problem of free riders—fixing the problem of the bottom billion would help everyone, so let's hope someone else does it. Without that mythical world government the major governments of the world have to work together to address the problem. The only forum for doing this at present is the G8. If the G8 imagines that it has fixed the problem of the bottom billion by doubling aid to Africa at the 2005 summit, it had better do a reality check. Aid alone is not going to resolve this problem. However, given the Gleneagles decision, the urgent matter is now to bring on the other three instruments—security, trade, and standards. These three were already neglected relative to aid even before aid was doubled. Now the imbalance is even more pronounced. Coordination on military interventions, trade policies, and international standards is going to be difficult because of recent history: coordination on military intervention is clouded by the spectacular disagreements over Iraq, coordination on trade policy is clouded by the spectacular disagreements on steel and agriculture, and coordination on international standards is clouded by the spectacular disagreements on climate change and the Kyoto Protocol. The recent track record is thus hardly propitious. However, the rich world has a strong collective interest in coordinating its policies to support the bottom billion regardless of its internal disagreements on these other matters. With proper leadership, cooperation on policies for the bottom billion—where there is little need for friction—could even reestablish the spirit of cooperation in other areas. The G8 meeting of 2007 in Germany is the next opportunity for coordinated leadership, and quite properly Africa is again on the agenda.

Problems of Focus

The Millennium Development Goals were in one sense a big advance. Compare them with an earlier UN jamboree, the Copenhagen Social Summit of 1995. The Social Summit ended with a clarion call about how much should be spent on social priorities. The Millennium Development Goals encouraged people to shift their agenda from inputs to outcomes: halving poverty, getting children in school, and so forth. But despite this advance, the goals have two weaknesses, both involving a lack of focus.

The first critical lack of focus is that the MDGs track the progress of five billion of the six billion people on our planet. It is of course politically easier for the United Nations to include almost everyone. Plus the aid agencies prefer a wide definition of the development challenge because that justifies a near-global role for their staff. The price we pay is that our efforts are spread too thin, and the strategies that are appropriate only for the countries at the bottom get lost in the general babble. It is time to redefine the development problem as being about the countries of the bottom billion, the ones that are stuck in poverty. When I give this message to audiences in aid agencies people shuffle uncomfortably in their seats. Some of them may be thinking, "But what about my career?" for it would no longer be in Rio but in Bangui. And when I give the message to an NGO audience they get uneasy for a different reason. Many of them do not want to believe that for the majority of the developing world global capitalism is working. They hate capitalism and do not want it to work. The news that it is not working for the billion at the bottom is not good enough: they want to believe that it does not work anywhere. But we cannot go on sacrificing the bottom billion to either of these self-serving aspirations.

The other critical lack of focus is on strategies to achieve the goals. Growth is not a cure-all, but the lack of growth is a kill-all. Over the past thirty years the bottom billion has missed out on global growth of unprecedented proportions. This failure of the growth process is the overwhelming problem that we have to crack. I have tried to show you how breaking the constraints upon growth will require a customized strategy. The same approach is not going to work everywhere, but neither is each country utterly distinctive. Governments in the countries of the bottom billion need to develop strategies appropriate for their circumstances. In principle, they do already—except that in practice their "strategies" are usually more like shopping lists presented to donors. This deformation of strategic thinking is in part a result of the overemphasis upon aid: the strategies turn into shopping lists because the objective is not growth but aid. The governments of the bottom billion need to become more ambitious.

What Can Ordinary People Do?

Our approach toward the bottom billion has been failing. Many of these societies are heading down, not up, and they are collectively diverging from the rest of the world. If we let this continue, our children are going to face an alarmingly divided world and all its consequences.

It does not have to be like that. The bottom billion are not condemned to slip in and out of war; they face a range of possible futures. Compared to the Cold War, the challenge of developing the bottom billion is scarcely daunting, but it does require us to get serious. That requires a change of attitude on the part of Western electorates, both left and right.

The left needs to move on from the West's self-flagellation and idealized notions of developing countries. Poverty is not romantic. The countries of the bottom billion are not there to pioneer experiments in socialism; they need to be helped along the already trodden path of building market economies. The international financial institutions are not part of a conspiracy against poor countries; they represent beleaguered efforts to help. The left has to learn to love growth. Aid cannot just be targeted for the photogenic social priorities; it has to be used to help countries break into export markets. At present the clarion call for the left is Jeffrey Sachs' book *The End of Poverty*. Much as I agree with Sachs' passionate call to action, I think that he has overplayed the importance of aid. Aid alone will not solve the problems of the bottom billion—we need to use a wider range of policies.

The right needs to move on from the notion of aid as part of the problem—as welfare payments to scroungers and crooks. It has to disabuse itself of the belief that growth is something that is always there for the taking, if only societies would get themselves together. It has to face up to the fact that these countries are stuck, that competing with China and India is going to be difficult. Indeed, it has to recognize that private activity in the global market can sometimes generate problems for the poorest countries that need public solutions. And because not even the U.S. government is big enough to fix these problems by itself, these public solutions will usually have to be cooperative. At present the clarion call for the right is economist William Easterly's book *The White Man's Burden*. Easterly is right to mock the delusions of the aid lobby. But just as Sachs exaggerates the payoff to aid, Easterly exaggerates the downside and again neglects the scope for other policies. We are not as impotent and ignorant as Easterly seems to think.

So how does this involve ordinary people in rich societies? Electorates tend to get the politicians they deserve. A classic example in the rich democracies is something called the "political business cycle." For years governments routinely spent money just before an election to artificially boost the economy, facing up to the consequent mess only once reelected. Eventually, electorates wised up to what was happening, and so the ploy no longer pulled in the votes. As a result, politicians now rarely try it. That sort of learning has to happen across the range of policies needed for the bottom billion. These shifts in thinking depend upon ordinary citizens—people who manage to read to the end of a book. Of course, in a book of this length I cannot set out all the evidence. But I hope that I have convinced you of three central propositions, each unfortunately fairly novel, that encapsulate how thinking needs to change.

The first is that the development problem we now face is not that of the past forty years: it is not the five billion people of the developing world and the Millennium Development Goals that track their progress. It is a much more focused problem of around a billion people in countries that are stuck. This is the problem we are going have to tackle, and if we stick with present efforts, it is likely to be intractable even as the dashboard indicators of world poverty get better and better.

The second is that within the societies of the bottom billion there is an intense struggle between brave people who are trying to achieve change and powerful groups who oppose them. The politics of the bottom billion is not the bland and sedate process of the rich democracies but rather a dangerous contest between moral extremes. The struggle for the future of the bottom billion is not a contest between an evil rich world and a noble poor world. It is within the societies of the bottom billion, and to date we have largely been bystanders.

The third is that we do not need to be bystanders. Our support for change can be decisive. But we will need not just a more intelligent approach to aid but complementary actions using instruments that have not conventionally been part of the development armory: trade policies, security strategies, changes in our laws, and new international charters.

In short, we need to narrow the target and broaden the instruments. That should be the agenda for the G8.

Research on Which
This Book Is Based

My current research is posted on my Web site, http://users.ox.ac.uk/~econpco.

Some of the publications on which the book is based are:

By the author

"Is Aid Oil? An Analysis of Whether Africa Can Absorb More Aid," *World Development* 34 (2006): 1482–97.

"Why the WTO Is Deadlocked: And What Can Be Done About It," *The World Economy* 29 (2006): 1423–49.

"Implications of Ethnic Diversity," *Economic Policy* 32 (2001): 127–55.

"African Growth: Why a 'Big Push'?" Journal of African Economics, 15, Supp. 2 (2006): 188–211.

With Anke Hoeffler

"Unintended Consequences: Does Aid Promote Arms Races?" *Oxford Bulletin of Economics and Statistics,* 2007: 69. 1–29.

"Military Expenditure in Post-Conflict Societies," *Economics of Governance* 7 (2006): 89–107.

"Greed and Grievance in Civil War," *Oxford Economic Papers* 54 (2004): 563–95.

"Aid, Policy, and Growth in Post-Conflict Societies," *European Economic Review* 48 (2004):, 1125–45.

"On the Incidence of Civil War in Africa," *Journal of Conflict Resolution* 46
(2002): 13–28.
"Aid, Policy, and Peace: Reducing the Risks of Civil Conflict," *Defence and Peace Economics* 13 (2002): 435–50.

With Stefan Dercon

"The Complementarities of Poverty, Equity and Growth," *Economic Development and Cultural Change* 55 (2006): 223–36.

With Catherine Pattillo

Investment and Risk in Africa (New York: St. Martin's Press, 2000).

With Anke Hoeffler and Catherine Pattillo

"Africa's Exodus: Capital Flight and the Brain Drain as Portfolio Decisions," *Journal of African Economics* 13, Supp. 2 (2004): 15–54.
"Capital Flight as a Portfolio Choice," *World Bank Economic Review* 15 (2001): 55–80.

With Anke Hoeffler and Måns Söderbom

"On the Duration of Civil War," *Journal of Peace Research* 41 (2004): 253–73.

With Lani Elliott, Harvard Hegre, Anke Hoeffler, Marta Reynol-Querol, and Nick Sambanis

Breaking the Conflict Trap (New York: Oxford University Press, 2003).

With Jan Gunning

"Explaining African Economic Performance," *Journal of Economic Literature* 37 (1999): 64–111.
"Why Has Africa Grown So Slowly?" *Journal of Economic Perspectives* 13 (1999): 3–22.
Trade Shocks in Developing Countries, Vol. 1; Africa (Oxford: Clarendon Press, 1999).

With David Dollar

Globalization, Growth and Poverty (New York: Oxford University Press, 2002).
"Aid Allocation and Poverty Reduction," *European Economic Review* 46 (2002):
1475–1500.

*With Arne Bigsten, Stefan Dercon, Marcel Fachamps, Bernard Gauthier,
Jan Willem Gunning, Abena Oduro, Remco Oostendorp Catherine Pattillo,
Måns Söderbom, Francis Teal, and Albert Zeufack*

"Do African Manufacturing Firms Learn from Exporting?" *Journal of Development
Studies* 40 (2004): 115–41.

Index

Abacha, Sani, 135–36
Administrative costs, 118
Afghanistan, 31, 146
Africa, ix, 67, 166–67, 181, 188. *See also*
      specific countries
   capital scarcity in, 87
   coups in, 36
   developmental problem centered in, 7
   diversifying exports of, 85
   failing countries concentrated in, 3
   G8 summit doubling aid to, 100, 138
   landlocked countries of, 57
African Economic Research Consortium, 84
African Growth Opportunity Act (AGOA), 83,
      168–69
African Peer Review Mechanism, 151
African Union, 130
Agency for International Development, 12
AGOA. *See* African Growth Opportunity Act
Aid
   absorption of, 101
   attracting, 62
   bottom billion receiving capital as, 87
   capital flight reduced by, 123
   concentration of, 122
   conflict trap relating to, 104–7
   coups encouraged by, 105, 180
   critique of, 40
   for development, 100, 134
   economic policies relating to, 102–3, 109
   economic reform after, 117–20
   effective provision of, 179
   export sector benefiting from, 121
   extortion v., 134
   G8 summit doubling, 100, 138

governance/policies relating to, 102–3,
      108–11
   as incentive, 108–11
   landlocked countries receiving, 107–
      8
   marginalization relating to, 120–22
   natural resource trap relating to, 107
   policy changes for, 183–84
   political disagreements over, 99–100
   postconflict societies receiving, 177
   prior to reform, 117–20
   providing, xi
   raising growth, 102
   as reinforcement, 115–17
   requirements for receiving, 67
   as skills, 111–15
   timing of, 106
   trade barriers relating to, 162–63
   World Bank disbursing, 109
Aid agencies, 4, 103–4
   bottom billion as focus of, 136–37
   concentration of, 184
   development assigned to, 12–13
   in failing states, 118
   fiefdoms of, 122
   opportunities for, 114–15
   risk in operations of, 117
AIDS, 31
Air transport, 60–61
Amin, Idi, 89, 155
Angola, 26, 28, 86–88
   oil companies, 141–42, 144–45
Annan, Kofi, 158
Asia, 167–70
Autocracy, 43, 47, 49–50

Banda, Hastings, 69
Bangladesh, 65, 68
Banks, 136
Bhagwati, Jagdish, 158
bin Laden, Osama, 31
Blair, Tony, 7, 138
Bono, 188
Boom-and-bust phenomenon, 40
Bosnia, 127
Botchwey, Kwesi, 181
Botswana, 50
Bottom billion, 11–12
    achieving/sustaining change, 139
    aid agencies focusing on, 136–37
    capital bypassing, 88–91
    capital inflow of, 87–91, 95
    capital outflow of, 91–93
    civil war in, 17–18
    coastal economy of, 121
    coups as problem for, 131
    democracy in, 71
    diverging from rest of world economy, 4
    economic policy in, 179, 191
    economic reform in, 143
    electoral competition in, 146
    export diversification as answer for, 166–67
    failing states in, 69
    global economy integrating, 93
    global market integrating, 86
    globalization consequences for, 81, 95
    governance in, 136, 179, 185
    governments of, 4–5, 190
    growth rates, 9–12, 35, 100
    improvement in, 9–10
    income in, 8–9
    life expectancy of, 7
    long-term malnutrition in, 8
    marginalization of, 79–96
    migration relating to, 93–95
    military spending in, 133
    moving toward change, 12
    new export markets of, 170
    oil revenue in, 101
    politicians in, 66–67
    raising growth in, 12
    reality of, 3
    risk of investment in, 88–89
    safe haven for, 135
    struggle within societies of, 192
    trade barriers in, 160–63
    trade relating to, 81–87
    traps v. limbo in, 96
    traps within, 37
    voting in, 45
    in WTO, 170–72
Brent Spar, 145
Bribery, 137, 148–49
British Commonwealth, 186
British Department of Trade and Industry, 12

Budget
    coups increasing, 133
    global aid, 32
    support, 101, 112
    transparency, 149–51, 180
Budget support, 101, 112
Burkina Faso, 53, 63
Bush, George W., 74–75, 110, 188

Capacity building, 112
Capital
    bypassing bottom billion, 88–91
    globalization providing, 87
    inflow of bottom billion, 87–91, 95
    outflow of bottom billion, 91–93
    scarcity in Africa, 87
    traps depressing return on, 92
Capital flight, 120–21, 123
Central African Republic, 4, 53, 55, 58
Central Asia, 3
Centre for Economic Policy Research, 158
Chad, 65–66, 119, 149
Chad-Cameroon oil pipeline, 119
Change(s), 12
    law, 185
    military intervention, 184
    postconflict potential for, 94
    in societies, xi
    support for, 192
    trade policy, 187
Charter
    for budget transparency, 149–51, 180
    for democracy, 146–49, 180
    for investment, 153–56, 183
    for natural resource revenue, 140–46
    for postconflict situations, 151–53, 178, 186
Chaudhry, Mahendra, 24
Chauvet, Lisa, 67, 73, 75, 111, 112–13, 118
Chávez, Hugo, 65
Checks and balances, 147–48
    in Nigeria, 48
    rents eroding, 46–47
China, 49, 66, 86, 120, 186
Christian Aid, 155, 157–59, 162, 163
Civil war, x
    in bottom billion, 17–18
    causes of, 18–26
    consequences of, 126
    costs of, 27–32
    emergence from, 70–72
    end of, 27
    ethnic dominance relating to, 25
    geography contributing to, 26
    low income causing, 19–20
    natural resources, 21–22
    persistence of, 26–27
    prediction of, 19
    slow growth causing, 20–22
    as trap, 17–18, 32

Clinton, Bill, 187
Coastal access, 59–60
Cold War, 124, 191
Commission for Africa, 7, 188
Commitment technologies, 155
Commonwealth Development Corporation, 24
Competition, 160–63
Conditionality, 67, 109–11
Conflict
  costs, 31
  postconflict military spending deterring, 132
  prevention, 178
  probability of, 128
  risk of reversion to, 153
Conflict diamonds, 21
Conflict oil, 144
Conflict trap, x, 32–36
  aid relating to, 104–7
  G8 policy relating to, 37
  points of intervention for, 177–78
Construction sector, 137–38
Consumer pressure, 146
Convergence, 80, 84, 164–65
Coordination, 187–89
Copenhagen Social Summit, 189
Corruption
  in construction sector, 137–38
  epicenters of, 137–38
  in money, 136, 138
Cost-benefit analysis, 32
Cost-competitiveness, 83
Costs
  administrative, 118
  of civil war, 27–32
  of failing states, 73–74, 114
  of military intervention, 74–75
  postwar, 28
  transport, for landlocked countries, 55
Côte d'Ivoire, 113, 129, 131
Country ownership, 108
Country Policy and Institutional Assessment, 67
Coups
  Africa as epicenter of, 36
  aid encouraging, 105, 180
  bottom billion problem with, 131
  causes of, 35
  in Central African Republic, 58
  military budget increased by, 133
  protection against, 129
Credibility, 90–91
Cross-border trade, 58
Cuba, 12

De Beers, 21, 136, 144
Debt relief, 102
Delocalization, 83
Democracy. *See also* Resource-rich democracy
  in bottom billion, 71
  campaign spending in, 149

charter for, 146–49, 180
  dysfunctional, 51
  electoral competition in, 47
  emphasizing political restraints, 50
  natural resources relating to, 43
  in Nigeria, 50
  oil relating to, 42–43
Democratic Republic of the Congo, 34, 55
Democratic rights, 37
Department for International Development,
  13, 187
Development, xi
  aid, 100, 134
  armory, 192
  assigned to aid agencies, 12–13
  biz/buzz, 4
  challenge, 3
  commission, 7
  failures, x
  global, xi
  gulf, 11
  ministry, 188
  problem, 192
  role of growth in, 8–13
  round, 171
  traps, 5–8, 13
Diamonds, 136, 144. *See also* Conflict diamonds
Diminishing returns, 100
Diogo, Luisa, 132
Discounted present value, 74
Discrimination, 24
Divergence, 10, 164–65
Dollar, David, 103
Domestic investors, 154–55
Domestic militaries, 131
Dutch disease, 39–40, 50, 56, 121
  diversifying exports hindered by, 178
  ending, 182
  offsetting, 122
  trade liberalization as remedy for, 163

East Timor, 127, 142
Easterly, William, 191
Eastern Europe, 139
EBA. *See* Everything but Arms
ECGD. *See* Export Credits Guarantee
  Department
Economic opportunities, 29–30, 66
Economic policies
  aid relating to, 102–3, 109
  in Bangladesh, 68
  in bottom billion, 179
  bottom billion requiring wider range of, 191
  conditionality of, 109
  growth process relating to, 64–65
  neighbors improving, 59
  opportunities relating to, 29–30, 66
  transforming, 79
  World Bank disbursing aid based on, 109

Economic reform
    aid prior to, 117–20
    in bottom billion, 143
    countries with strongest, 89
    educated people implementing, 71
    in failing states, 72–73, 180–82
    failure of, 85
    growth induced by, 41
    money as counterproductive for, 115–16
    in Nigeria, 64–65
    political difficulty of, 90
    skills required for, 111–15
    technical assistance in, 114
    technicality of, 67
    Zimbabwe launching, 109
Economic success, 47
Economics, ix, 17
Economies of agglomeration, 82
Economy
    risk according to, 34
    weakness, 21
Education, 93–94
Electoral competition
    in bottom billion, 146
    bribery in, 45
    in democracy, 47
    growth blockage overcome by, 50
    rents altering, 44
    unrestrained, 49
Embezzlement, 45
Emigration, 61, 94, 121
Employment policies, 145
The End of Poverty (Sachs), 191
Environmental damage, 31
Environmental policies, 145
Equatorial Guinea, 10
Eritrea, 138
E-services, 60–61
Ethiopia, 113
Ethnic diversity, 49
Ethnic dominance, 25
Ethnic loyalties, 45
Ethnic minorities, 23
European Commission, 104, 186
European Union, 80, 139, 147, 164–65, 170
Everything but Arms (EBA), 168–69
Export Credits Guarantee Department
    (ECGD), 154
Export diversification, 85, 87, 120
    as answer for bottom billion, 166–67
    beginning, 167–70
    Dutch Disease hindering, 178
Extortion
    aid v., 134
    grand, 133
Extractive Industries Transparency Initiative,
    138, 140–41, 143, 178–79, 185
Eyadéma, Gnassingbé, 130

Facilitation payment, 137
Failing states, 68
    aid agencies in, 118
    in bottom billion, 69
    costs of, 73–74, 114
    economic reform in, 72–73, 180–82
    G8 policy relating to, 73–75
    growth rate of, 74
    technical assistance in, 113–14
    turnarounds in, 69
Failure. *See also* Failing states
    growth, 190
    of reforms, 85
    societies learning from, 66
False consciousness, 41
Fearon, Jim, 23
Fiefdoms, 122
Focus, 189–90
Foreign currency, 91, 162
France, 113
Free press, 48
Freedom House, 48
Fujimori, Alberto, 148
Future-generations fund, 142

G8
    agenda, 13, 192
    doubling aid to Africa, 100, 138
    governments coordinated by, 189
    summit, 100, 121, 138
G8 policy, 62
    conflict trap relating to, 37
    failing states relating to, 73–75
    natural resource trap relating to, 52
Geography, 26, 54
Githongo, John, 181
Global aid budget, 32
Global capitalism, 5
Global Corruption Report 2005, 138
Global economic system, x, 93
Global market
    bottom billion joining, 86
    breaking into, 83
    hostility of, 6
    resource-scarce economies joining, 85
Global poverty, x, 191
    low income meaning, 20
    reduction, xii, 11
    resource wealth contributing to, 39
Global public goods, 156
Globalization, 6, 88, 175
    capital provided by, 87
    consequences for bottom billion, 81, 95
    opportunities provided by, 10
    ramifications on developing countries, 80
Governance
    aid relating to, 102–3, 108–11
    in Bangladesh, 68

in bottom billion, 136, 179, 185
conditionality, 110
growth process relating to, 64–65
of oil revenues, 142–43
opportunities relating to, 66
transforming, 79
Governments
of bottom billion countries, 4–5, 190
coordinating range of policies, xi
coordination between multiple, 188–89
discrimination perpetrated by, 24
intentions signaled by, 90–91
military spending controlled by, 132
transforming money into public services, 66
treatment of investors, 153
Grand extortion, 133
Greenaway, David, 159
Grievances, 18, 22
awareness of, 30
flagrant, 24
Growth, 8–13
aid raising, 102
in Botswana, 50
Burkina Faso/Uganda sustaining rates of, 63
civil war resulting from slow, 20–22
development role of, 8–13
economic policies/governance relating to, 64–65
economic reform inducing, 41
electoral competition overcoming blockage to, 50
ethnic diversity relating to, 49
failure of, 190
lack of, leading to civil war, 20–22
in landlocked countries, 56
natural resource wealth harnessed for, 38
oil lowering, 102
population, 6
rate of bottom billion, 9–12, 35, 100
rate of failing states, 74
reducing risk, 32, 106
spilling over from neighbors, 58–59
strategy, 58
"Growth is Good for the Poor," 11
Gueï, Robert, 129

Hegre, Harvard, 34
Hoeffler, Anke, 17, 23, 33, 91, 93, 103–4, 123, 127, 132–33, 152
Homicide rate, 34
Hope, 9
Hopelessness, 20
Human capital, 93
Human Development Index, 25
Hussein, Saddam, 42, 49, 51, 75

IBRD. See International Bank for Reconstruction and Development

IDA. See International Development Association
Images, xii
IMF. See International Monetary Fund
Immigration, 61
Import restrictions, 169
Improvement
policy, 90
sustained, 70, 139
Income, 7
in bottom billion, 8–9
gap, 10
generated by primary commodity exporting, 81
inequality, 23–24
level to ensure safety, 99
low, 26
relating to war, 19–20
resource surplus increasing, 44
Independent service authority, 118, 120
India, 60, 120
Indonesia, 92
Industrial Surveys of Africa, 166–67
Industrialization, 62
Infrastructure, 59, 108, 121, 138
Institutional Investor, 89, 92–93
International arbitration, 154
International Bank for Reconstruction and Development (IBRD), 171
International charters, 139
opposition of, 182
promulgation of, 185
International Development Association (IDA), 171–72
International insurance, 154
International Monetary Fund (IMF), 8, 40, 58, 67, 186
International standards, 140, 143
Interventions, 72. See also Military intervention
cost of military, 74–75
at end of Cold War, 106
nonmilitary, 75
Investment
charter for, 153–56
laws encouraging private, 183
rate of v. return on, 44
IRA. See Irish Republican Army
Iraq, 52, 74–75, 124–25
Irish Republican Army (IRA), 22
Italy, 113

Kabila, Laurent, 21
Kalashnikovs, 33
KANU. See Kenya African National Union
Kenya, 40, 108, 181
Kenya African National Union (KANU), 181
Kenyan coffee boom, 40
Kibaki, Mwai, 181
Killicoat, Phil, 33

Kimberley Process, 179
Köhler, Horst, 7
Krugman, Paul, 54, 82, 122
Kuwait, 38, 124–25

Laitin, David, 23
Landlocked countries, 79
  of Africa, 57
  aid for, 107–8
  growth in, 56
  lifelines for, 179–80
  neighboring markets accessed by, 165
  neighbors of, 54
  resource-scarce, 57, 62–63
  transport costs for, 55
Laws
  changing, 156
  encouraging private investment, 183
  mobilizing changes in, 185
  problems caused by, 135–36
Liberation, 23
Limbo, 96, 182
"Look east" strategy, 86
Lord's Resistance Army, 28

Madagascar, 83–84, 161, 169, 183
Malawi, 69
Malaysia, 88
Malnutrition, 8
Manufacturing, 160–62
Mao Zedong, 66
Marginalization, 79–96, 120–22
Mauritius, 85
McMillan, John, 148
McMillan, Maggie, 140
Media, 67, 147, 148, 150
Middle East, 92
MIGA. See Multilateral Investment Guarantee
    Agency
Migration, 93–95
Military dictatorship, 48
Military intervention, 179
  arousing support for, 124
  mobilizing changes in, 184
  opportunities for, 128–29
  in Somalia, 125–26
Military spending, 103
  coups increasing, 133
  government controlling, 132
  postconflict, 27
Millennium Challenge Account, 110, 188
Millennium Development Goals, 3, 11, 189, 192
Minimal state, 65
Ministry of Finance, 150
Moi, Daniel Arap, 181
Money
  alternative system for spending public, 119
  corrupt, 136, 138
  counterproductivity for reform of, 115–16

governments transforming into public
    services, 66
  technical assistance relating to, 116
Montesinos, Vladimiro, 148
Mozambican National Resistance (RENAMO),
    29
MPLA. See Popular Movement for the Liberation
    of Angola
Mugabe, Robert, 64, 86, 155, 185
Multilateral Investment Guarantee Agency
    (MIGA), 154–55

National Union for the Total Independence of
    Angola (UNITA), 26, 28, 87
Natural resource trap, 50–52
  aid relating to, 107
  avoiding problems of, 62
  breaking, 115, 178–79
  G8 policy relating to, 52
  understanding, 38–39
Natural resources
  charter for revenues of, 140–46
  civil war influenced by, 21–22
  cleaning up revenues from, 144
  democracy relating to, 43
  dependence upon, 175
  depletion of, 79
  financing public services, 140
  harnessed for growth, 38
  landlocked countries scarce in, 57, 62–63
  poverty created by, 39
  rebellion motivated by, 30, 105
  securing supplies of, 86
  societies rich in, 42
  surpluses of, 43
  volatile revenues of, 40
  war over, 26
Neighbors, 54
  benefiting from, 56
  growth spillovers from, 58–59
  improving economic policies of, 59
  landlocked countries accessing markets of,
    165
  as markets, 55
NGO (Non-governmental organization), 155,
    157, 159, 185, 187
Nigeria, 30, 39, 116, 144, 151, 180
  checks and balances in, 48
  democracy in, 50
  oil crash in, 40–41
  reform phase of, 64–65
  World Bank perceived by, 41
Non-governmental organization. See NGO
Norms, 139

Obasanjo, Olusegun, 48
O'Connell, Steve, 56, 84
OECD. See Organisation for Economic
    Co-operation and Development

Oil
in Angola, 141–42, 144–45
companies bearing price risk, 140–41
crash in Nigeria, 40–41
crash in world prices of, 65
democracy relating to, 42–43
governance of revenues from, 142–43
growth lowered by, 102
in Middle East, 52
revenue in bottom billion, 101
Okonjo-Iweala, Ngozi, 116, 150, 161
Operation Palliser, 127–28
OPIC. *See* Overseas Private Investment
Corporation
Organisation for Economic Co-operation and
Development (OECD), 112, 137, 151,
155, 185
tariffs imposed by, 168
trade policy of, 159–60
Outsourcing. *See* Delocalization
Overseas Private Investment Corporation
(OPIC), 154
Oxford Revolutionary Socialist Students, ix
Oyefusi, Aderoju, 30

Patronage politics, 45–46
Pattillo, Cathy, 88, 91, 93, 123
Peace, 131
Peace-Building Commission, 186
Pearson Commission, 7
Perpetual inventory method, 92
Philippines, 61
Policy incoherence, 160
Policy instruments, 12
Political business cycle, 192
Political development trap, 51
Political divide, xi–xii
Political restraints
democracy emphasizing, 50
enthusiasm for, 147
on power, 47
as public good, 51
resource revenues weakening, 46
Political rights, 23
Politicians, 24, 66–67
Politics
arguments in, regarding aid, 99–100
conflict inherent in, 17
patronage, 45–46
resource surplus relating to, 44
Popular Movement for the Liberation of Angola
(MPLA), 26
Population
growth, 6
turnaround influenced by, 70–72
Portfolio choice, 92
Postconflict, 27
aid, 177
charter for, situations, 151–53, 178, 186

countries sustaining turnaround, 72–73
crime in, society, 33
maintaining peace, 126–29
military spending deterring conflict, 132
political evolution, 152
potential for change, 94
relapses, 34
reverting to conflict, 131
security for, societies, 177–78
situations, high risk in, 133
Postwar costs, 28
Poverty. *See* Global poverty
Poverty efficiency, 104
Power
political restraints on, 47
use of, 147
Primary commodity exporting, 81
Private Capital Inflows, 88–91, 95. *See also*
Capital
Private Capital Outflows, 91–93. *See also*
Capital
Private investment, 87
Public expenditure, 44
Public investment project, 48
Public opinion, 183–84
Public service provisions, 46, 120
government providing, 66
natural resources financing, 140
Public spending, 141–42
Purpose, xii

Qaddafi, Muammar, 21

Rajan, Raghuram, 121
Rapid reaction force, 129–30
Ratsiraka, Didier, 83
Ravalomanana, Marc, 161
Reagan, Ronald, 67
Rebel group. *See* Rebel movements
Rebel movements
challenges for, 132
flagrant grievances held by, 24
funding for, 22
justification of, 18
recruitment for, 29–30
Refugees, 28
Regional haven, 60
Regional integration, 164–66
Reinikka, Ritva, 150
Relapse, 27, 34
Remittances, 61
RENAMO. *See* Mozambican National
Resistance
Rents, 38, 41, 147
altering electoral competition, 44
checks and balances eroded by, 46–47
estimating, 43
Republic of the Congo, 21
Research, xii–xiii, 18

Resource. *See also* Natural resources
  discoveries, 9–10
  extraction, 137–38
  prospecting, 61
  revenues, 46
Resource curse, 39
  heart of, 42
  shifting, 52
Resource surplus
  increasing income, 44
  politics relating to, 44
Resource-rich democracy, 44
  dangers facing, 49
  as economic success, 47
  underperformance of, 44
Revolutionary United Front (RUF), 29
Reynol-Querol, Marta, 28
Rich-countries, 157
Risk, 20, 32
  according to economy, 34
  growth reducing, 32, 106
  high in postconflict situations, 133
  of investing in bottom billion,
    88–89
  investment opportunities with high, 92
  in operations of aid agencies, 117
  perceived by resource extraction companies,
    61
  price, 140–41
  rating reflecting turnaround, 89
  ratings of Uganda, 89
  in rebellions/coups, 105
  of reversion to conflict, 153
ROOs. *See* Rules of origin
Root causes, 22
RUF. *See* Revolutionary United Front
Rules of origin (ROOs), 169
Rwanda, 125

Sachs, Jeffrey, 5, 41, 54, 105, 191
Sahel, 180
Sankoh, Foday, 25, 28
Saro-Wiwa, Ken, 30
Sassou-Nguesso, Denis, 21
Savimbi, Jonas, 28, 87
School of Oriental and African Studies, 158
Secondary education, 70–72
Security, 177–78
Seko, Mobutu Sese, 155
Selection by intrinsic motivation, 111
Sembet, Lemma, 94
Shagari, Shehu, 48
Short, Clare, 159, 184
Sierra Leone, 25, 29, 127–29
Skills, 111–15
Society
  change in, xi
  conflicts of, 17
  crime in postconflict, 33–34

failure informing, 66
  fragility of, 33
  rescued from within, 96
  resource-rich, 42
  struggle within bottom billion, 192
Socioeconomic data, 18
Söderbom, Måns, 152
Soludo, Charles, 151, 180
Somalia, 25, 94, 125–26
South Africa, 152
Specialization, x
Speight, George, 24–25
Stiglitz, Joe, ix, xi
Stockholm Peace Research Institute, 103
Structural adjustment program, 41
Supervision, 118
Svensson, Jakob, 150
Switzerland, 55, 56–57

Tamil Tigers, 22
Tariff escalation, 160
Tariffs
  escalation of, 160
  OECD imposing, 168
Technical assistance, 112
  delivery of, 181
  in economic reform, 114
  as emergency relief, 115
  in failing states, 113–14
  money relating to, 116
Thatcher, Margaret, 67
Third world, 3
Togo, 130
Trade
  advocacy, 157–58
  barriers, 160–63, 171
  fair, 163
  free, 164
  liberalization, 161, 163
  relating to bottom billion, 81–87
  restrictions, 82
  technology of, 60–61
Trade policy, 59, 159–60
  changing, 122, 187
  Christian Aid campaign for, 157–59
  mobilizing changes in, 187
  rich-country, 159–60
Transparency International, 65
Transport infrastructure, 59
Traps
  within bottom billion, 37
  defining, 5–8
  development, 5–8, 13
  emerging from, 80, 95
  future, 95–96
  instruments for escaping, 176
  probability of, 79
  return on capital influenced by, 92
  war as, 17–18, 32

Troops
  British, 127–28
  danger for, 125, 127
  peacekeeping, 126
Tumusiime-Mutebile, Emmanuel, 150, 161
Turnarounds
  aborting, 90
  in failing states, 69
  incipient, 71–72
  population influencing, 70–72
  in postconflict countries, 72–73
  preconditions for, 70–71
  risk ratings reflecting, 89
  statistics of, 69–70
  value of successful, 75
  World Bank supporting, 117

Uganda, 55, 57, 59, 150, 166
  link to coast, 108
  risk ratings of, 89
  sustained growth rates in, 63
UN peacekeepers, 127
Underinvesting, 44
UNITA. *See* National Union for the Total
    Independence of Angola
United Nations, 3, 19, 127–29, 186, 190
U.S. Department of Defense, 12
USAID, 110

Venables, Tony, 54, 82, 122, 158–59, 164
Venture aid fund, 117
Venture capital fund, 117

Violent crime, 34
Voting, 45. *See also* Electoral competition
  in bottom billion, 45
  cost-effective increase in, 47

Wage gap, 84
War. *See also* Civil war
  anticipation of, 20
  economic damage relating to, 33
  natural resource, 26
  risk of, 19
Weinstein, Jeremy, 29
The White Man's Burden (Easterly), 191
"Whole-of-government" approach, 13
Wolfensohn, Jim, 11
World Bank, ix, 58, 65
  disbursing aid, 109
  involvement in political matters, 186
  as mutual assistance organization, 171
  Nigerian perception of, 41
  offices of, 4
  protection from political influence on, 104
  research department, 11, 53
  supporting turnarounds, 117
World Economic Outlook, 8
World government, 183
World Trade Organization (WTO), 4, 155, 160,
    170–72
World War II, 176
WTO. *See* World Trade Organization

Zimbabwe, 64, 86, 109